One Foot in
Front of the Other

One Foot in Front of the Other

How I Survived Being Alone and Homeless on the Streets of Paris

Ann Webb

Skyhorse Publishing

Skyhorse Publishing books may be purchased in bulk at special discounts for sales
promotion, corporate gifts, fund-raising, or educational purposes. Special editions can also
be created to specifications. For details, contact the Special Sales Department, Skyhorse
Publishing, 307 West 36th Street, 11th Floor, New York, NY 10018 or
info@skyhorsepublishing.com.

Skyhorse® and Skyhorse Publishing® are registered trademarks of
Skyhorse Publishing, Inc.®, a Delaware corporation.

www.skyhorsepublishing.com

10 9 8 7 6 5 4 3 2 1

Library of Congress Cataloging-in-Publication Data is available on file.
ISBN: 978-1-62087-088-4

Printed in the United States of America

A collaboration with **Ruth Marshall**

Edited by **Francis Esmènard**
with **Patrice van Eersel**

In loving memory of my mother

Some names have been changed to protect people, and some dates have been slightly altered to keep the story moving forward.

This book is dedicated to homeless people all over the world. What I lived through is only a glimpse of their lives and what they endure every day to survive.

CONTENTS

Foreword

I never thought much about becoming homeless. It just didn't seem like something that could actually happen to me, but now I know it can happen to almost anyone, anytime, anywhere, and when you least expect it.

Being homeless is brutal. It strips you of all you have and everything you believe you are; it breaks you down to your core.

While I was on my dream vacation, I became stuck in Paris, France, and ended up homeless on the street. Paris has a very dark side most people never see.

On the tourist side, it's the fashion capital of the world with mesmerizing attractions like the Eiffel Tower and the Louvre. But if you dare venture into the other side, you will discover thousands of very cleverly disguised homeless people, living in a dangerous and sinister world you would not imagine existed, hidden within this grand, picturesque tourist capital of the world.

I started reading books by Eckhart Tolle in the fall of 2008. Thanks in part to these incredible books, I have started rebuilding myself from the core up. It is my belief that what I learned from these books enabled me to survive this series of unlikely events, and I continue to learn and practice their teachings. This is a true story that started as a struggle for survival and transformed into a spiritual journey.

This was my wake-up call.

"Dream Vacation"

It is very complicated to be homeless, but it is also very simple.

You put one foot in front of the other.

You stop worrying.

You discover that no matter where you are, you are not alone in the world.

⚜ ⚜ ⚜

It was around two in the morning and I was walking along the river, heading back from the Eiffel Tower toward the Louvre. It was very cold and there was fog rising off the water. My pants were already wet from sitting down on a bench. I'd been walking the streets of Paris for three nights and it didn't seem like I could keep going, so I took a rest on a bench and kind of half fell asleep, I guess. But I woke up quickly when a guy sat down beside me. He said something in French. I couldn't understand him, but I knew I'd have to shake him off, because I'd been doing this for long enough now to know that. So until eight in the morning, when the free hot shower place over by the Centre Pompidou opened, I'd just have to keep moving.

There's a great peace in walking; you're in pain, your feet and legs hurt, your body aches, and maybe you're hungry, but walking you'll sometimes find you settle into a steady rhythm. You're not thinking about anything special—walking helps cut down on unnecessary thinking—you just keep moving, one foot in front of the other, a good slow cadence, nice and calm. Your breathing kind of slows to fit in and you feel a sense of awareness that has nothing to do with the pain in your feet or your legs or your belly. Everything is going to be OK. You just have to keep going.

⚜ ⚜ ⚜

I used to be a nursing assistant in Portland, Oregon, and my life was kind of ordinary, though I don't mean that in a bad way. I was born in Shreveport, Louisiana, in 1965 and back then it was just a normal sort of town. There's an airbase, but until they got riverboat gambling going and started celebrating Mardi Gras for tourists, it was actually kind of bland. There were a lot of beauty pageants, and a couple of times when I was growing up there was a girl from Shreveport competing for Miss America.

My dad was a geologist and my mom was a homemaker. They met at a skating rink when she was sixteen and my dad was twenty-four. He was stationed at the airbase and she looked like Elizabeth Taylor. They got married a couple of years later.

My parents didn't push me to go to college, and if I did, I had to pay for it myself—my dad made that clear. He always expected me to work, as far back as I remember. If I wanted to get an allowance, I earned it—I had chores to do, and it couldn't be a halfway-done job I did, either.

I didn't start college until I was twenty-three, and I ended up getting an associate degree in microbiology at Louisiana Tech in Ruston. I really love looking through a microscope—it's like a whole other world opens up that's been with you the whole time but you never knew it was there. But after a few years, I stopped going to college full time. At first I was working as a waitress to put myself through school, but then I got a qualification as a nursing assistant, and I liked the work, and I got married. Then I got offered a job at a home-health-care agency in Monroe, but it was full time, and I guess it was all a bit much—marriage, a job, and going to school as well.

Then my mom died, on December 10, 1997. That was hard, and there were a lot of bad feelings. My father married another woman shortly after my mom died, and it turned out he had known her intimately for some years. I had two sisters and a brother, and our father said we had to accept this woman as our new mother—this stranger was suddenly family. But at that moment in my life, I couldn't; I needed time to grieve the loss of my mother. I signed some papers and basically cut ties with my dad. My sisters and brother became very angry with me when I signed these papers. Our perception of what was happening was obviously different. I felt the need to protect my mother's memory. In my mind she would always be sacred, and I believed my father's actions so soon after her death were disrespectful to her memory. I was going through a rough time: I guess my husband and I just grew apart, and I'd always wanted to live up north.

I kept thinking about one of my mother's favorite phrases: "If you want to do something, you'll never know if you can do it unless you try." Like one time, when I was seven or eight, there was a sports day at school and I was scared to enter the baton-twirling competition because there was a real pretty girl who was popular and won everything, and I just knew she'd win. My mom told me, "Think of the Cowardly Lion from *The Wizard of Oz*. Remember how happy he was once he realized he had courage?" So I entered the baton-twirling contest, and I ended up actually winning.

After she died, I thought about that, about courage and about dreams, and if I was going to move up north, it seemed like it was the right time to go.

I went to college with a girl from Portland. She always said it was beautiful up there in Oregon. You drove an hour one way and you were at the beach, an hour and a half the other way and you were in the mountains where it was snowing. So in 1999 I drove across the country with my cat to Oregon, way over between California and Canada, on the West Coast. I'd rented an apartment in Portland, sight unseen, and it was OK. I found work as a nursing assistant right away. Maybe it's something to do with the work ethic my parents taught me as a child, but I never had any trouble finding work.

I called, wrote, and sent Christmas cards to both my sisters and my brother for over two years after I moved, with my mailing address, and I never heard back from them. It was obvious they had made their choice, and I made mine to move forward.

It is my belief they never forgave me for signing the papers. They involved our mother's inheritance and my brother and sisters had signed the papers first, but since I was the last child to sign them, my signature made them official. Before I left they told me that the only reason they signed the papers was because they knew I *never* would, but they didn't communicate that until after I signed.

I don't believe the papers were legally notarized, because our father's new wife was a notary public, so he said she would make them legal by notarizing them, but it should have been a conflict of interest, considering her position. It was all a big mess, and I decided my mother's memory was worth more to me than any amount of money, so I let go of everything and everyone, and I left without a cent of my inheritance.

⚜ ⚜ ⚜

After I'd been living in Portland for a while, I started renting a room from another nursing assistant, Chloe. She lived in a townhouse in a development on 122nd and Division Street with her Mexican boyfriend, Carlos, and his brother had the other spare bedroom. It was only $400 a month—plus electric, cable etc.—a really great deal. I liked living with Chloe. It was fun to hang out together if we were both off work the same day, and we planted a vegetable garden outside the back door and grew tomatoes, hot peppers, and cilantro, and sometimes we'd barbecue. Carlos used to be a welder in Mexico and now he just worked stacking fruit in a supermarket, but he was a really great cook, and we had fun.

There was this homeless guy, Dean. The building manager let him have an apartment in return for doing maintenance and yard work. We used to save him bottles to recycle—you got five cents for every bottle you brought in—and if we were throwing something out, we'd give it to him to sell. He used to bring us things he'd found on the street. One time he gave Chloe a big yellow canvas canopy. I remember coming home from work and this thing was lying out there in front of the house and she was laughing and struggling to put it up. She and I finally assembled it, but the top kept caving in, so we puffed it up by opening a big outdoor umbrella underneath it. What a sight!

I had never left America before all this happened. I almost never took a vacation, just a day at the beach and get back in the evening, that kind of thing. I never had enough money for hotels and stuff. I lived paycheck to paycheck, always worked Christmas Day and New Year's Eve, just trying to make the bills. It was the same with almost everyone I knew. A lot of people around the world think all Americans are wealthy, but they really aren't.

But I liked my work. Being a nursing assistant is tough on your body and it can be difficult emotionally, but I felt useful. I knew *why* I was working, if you know what I mean. I used to work primarily through a nursing agency. You could make about sixteen dollars an hour that way, which was pretty good money, and I liked having the variety. When you're getting work through an agency, you might be working in a group home, maybe with severely autistic kids, or in an assisted-living center with up to a hundred elderly people, some of them with mild Alzheimer's. Or it could be in a hospital, in oncology or emergency or whatever department, or with elderly and disabled people in a nursing home.

You can really burn out working in a nursing home. A lot of them just don't have the resources they should. They'll run out of supplies, like not having any incontinence pads to put on the beds. When that happens, some of the patients will urinate right through their Attends—even though they are like adult diapers, it is forbidden to call them that—so you'll have to wake the poor person up to change the sheets, because they're soaked in urine. Or the nursing home will be understaffed, and you won't have time to take care of the patients the way you'd like to; you have to rush them around.

Sometimes it's kind of stressful and really sad. The patients start seeming more like objects on an assembly line than people, and the work is really tough on your back. There's a lot of lifting: Most of these people can barely stand, so you're lifting a lot of their weight.

If you're the nurse's aide, you get everyone up, bathe some, dress them, change Attends or toilet them—it's a state law that everyone that is continent has to be toileted every two hours. You pass the breakfast trays out and feed the patients who can't do it themselves. Then by the time you've toileted and changed them all again, and put some of them down for naps, it's time to prepare for lunch. It's hard, physical work: You're bending over and walking and lifting a lot. Your feet, legs, and back get really sore, and the work can be rough. In one of the group homes where I worked, one autistic kid, who was fourteen, broke a nurse's jaw when she was tying his shoe. He kicked her in the face, and her jaw had to be wired shut for six weeks. This kid was really difficult—he also broke a male nursing assistant's nose.

If you're a certified medication aide (CMA), you give out medications, and that can be a challenging task if the place you're working at doesn't keep its medical records well organized. You're giving five to ten pills each to maybe thirty people, sometimes as many as sixty to seventy people, and there are two or three med passes per shift, so you need to be able to identify who is who.

There are hospitals, home-health-care positions, nursing homes, assisted-living centers, and clinics that all need people to run tests: cardio, cholesterol, bone density, blood sugar, allergies, and so on. Everyone needs nursing assistants. If you work through a nursing agency, you can sort of choose, like, "Don't book me there for a couple of weeks, I need a break from that place." That way the work doesn't get you down so much.

But there's no paid sick leave or vacation time, and you're on your own for medical insurance.

That's crazy, huh? You're working in health care, but you don't get any medical insurance.

I remember one time at this nursing home where I was working evening shift as a CMA, a resident was sent to the hospital during the night and returned on my shift. The charge nurse instructed the certified nursing assistant (CNA) to take vital signs. This is normal protocol. He was just brought into the building by the ambulance staff. The CNA returned and said, "I can't take vital signs on this resident." The charge nurse asked why. The CNA replied, "Because he doesn't have any!" The man was dead! Apparently he died en route back to the nursing home. We ran outside and caught the ambulance staff, explaining that they had brought a dead man back from the hospital. They said, "Well, he's yours now. He's in your building, that's too much paperwork for us to fill out." A fine example of the American health-care system.

⚜ ⚜ ⚜

My life in Portland was OK. My husband even came up and we tried to work things out for a while, but I had changed after my mom died. After we eventually separated for good, I wanted to start something new. I wanted to experience different cultures, and to travel, really start living in the here and now. There were a few people around me telling stories about traveling around the world. One was the sister of a nurse I knew. She just saved and saved her money, and she never felt like she had enough, and then one day she said, "I'm just going to do it," and she took off. She went traveling to Mexico, Argentina, and Brazil—all over the place. I dreamed about doing things like that. I wanted to see the world, learn about new cultures, and have adventures.

Then one day, Maureen, who was a nurse at a group home where I frequently worked, told me that her daughter wasn't getting married anymore. Maureen was going to have to go on eBay and sell the time-share reservation she bought her daughter for a wedding present. It was a reservation for a two-week vacation at a condo in Spain, and Maureen said it was $600, which seemed like a great deal. I thought about it for a little while and then I told her to hold off on the eBay thing, because maybe I'd take it. I thought, *If I don't do it now, when is it going to happen?*

It would be like a little adventure, two weeks, maybe even three, and perhaps I could couch-surf like my friend's sister had. I could make my money stretch that way and get to travel around, see Paris, and maybe even London. It was something I wanted to do in this lifetime.

I went over to Maureen's house and she showed me the website where she rented the condo. The photos were great and she told me everyone she knew who'd ever been to Spain said it was beautiful, just amazing, you had to go. I asked her why she didn't go there herself and she said she didn't have any more time off, plus with the airfare there was no way she could afford it.

Wikipedia said Marbella, where the condo was located, was "a beach resort for the rich and famous" on the Costa del Sol. I wasn't sure where *that* was, I just saw a nice-looking beach by the blue sea, and then I looked at Paris. It didn't seem far.

I don't know if you ever heard a song by Marianne Faithfull:

> *At the age of thirty-seven, she realized she'd never ride through Paris, in a sports car, with the warm wind in her hair.*

Well, that's kind of the way I felt. I wasn't thirty-seven and I wasn't planning on any kind of sports car, but I figured it was time.

⚜ ⚜ ⚜

I started checking out airfares. It seemed like you could get to Europe and back for $1,500. I was making about that much a month after taxes, but I never had much money to spare after I paid my bills at the end of the month. I had a lot of bills: school loans, medication, car insurance, health club fees, a video store membership, and of course rent, electric, etc. So, at $1,500 airfare, plus $600 for the condo, it wasn't going to be easy paying for this trip.

But like my mom used to say, "If you want to do something, you'll never know unless you try. You must be brave and have courage."

I had time. All this was happening back in February or March 2008, and I had until December to use the time-share. I figured I needed to leave myself enough time to make the money, but I wanted to be back before Thanksgiving, because Carlos was already talking about making a spicy Mexican turkey, and Chloe and I had already talked about decorating the apartment for the holidays. My mom always loved holiday decorations. She used to keep boxes of them in the attic and I guess I'm like her. I especially love those little strings of Christmas lights. At Chloe's place, I put some up in my bedroom. They made a real soothing atmosphere. Chloe told me she had a fiber-optic Christmas tree in storage and we had talked about putting that up this year. I was looking forward to doing that.

So I decided to leave at the end of October. By then I calculated I should be able to make enough, doing double shifts when I could get them, to pay for the trip. Or I could pick up a second job. I had done that before, and a lot of people I knew had to work two jobs all the time just to make the bills. One girl used to work evening shift at a nursing home—from two to ten thirty—and then graveyard shift at the hospital, eleven to seven. She did that five nights a week. Sure, she was tired, but you've got to pay the bills. Another woman did laundry at the Holiday Inn during the daytime and then she worked the evening shift at an assisted-living facility.

At first I planned to find some friends to share the condo with me and split the costs, so we could see Europe together, but Chloe said there was no way she could get that much time off work, and I knew it was true. She was a team leader at a group home, and she probably got five or ten days vacation a year. Same with my friend Sara, who worked in the cardio unit of a local hospital full time: She went to school at night so she could get qualified to do medical transcription. And my friend Tammy worked at two different nursing homes, about sixty-four to seventy-two hours a week. She said she couldn't get away from work, either.

It was a little scary to be going on my own, but I was thinking positive: It would be like a real adventure. I'm very adaptable, a problem-solver, and I can deal with being on my own. In my line of work, I was put in challenging situations almost every day, so I felt I could handle it.

⚜ ⚜ ⚜

When I left, I had a one-way ticket that cost $600. Later I found out they're not supposed to let you fly on a one-way ticket—it's against the regulations if you don't have a visa—but the travel agency said it would be fine. I told them I was planning to wing it in Europe, spend two weeks at the condo in Spain, then see if I could get some couch-surfing going, and try to make it up to Paris, maybe even get to London.

They said if I bought a round-trip ticket and changed the return date, there would be extra charges, so I'd be better off waiting and buying the return ticket when I was ready to fix the date. I did some research. I'd met this guy who'd been to Europe recently, and I asked him about plane tickets, and I also asked my Chilean friend Alex, who's been all over the world. They both said when you're traveling, winging it is the best way. I could fly to Madrid, take the train to Marbella, spend two weeks at the condo, and kind of play it by ear from there.

I checked whether my prepaid credit card would operate in Europe, and the website said it would be fine. I used to get my paychecks put straight onto a prepaid credit card. It was a new system the nursing agency was encouraging us to use, and it worked pretty well. You didn't have to go pick up your check every week, and you never spent more money than you had.

I didn't have a normal bank account, because it never really seemed necessary. In America there are so many places where you can cash a check that you don't really need a bank account, and I was living paycheck to paycheck, so it wasn't like I had any savings. And regular credit cards are bad. You spend money you don't have, pay high interest rates, and get into debt. A lot of people I knew got into bad trouble that way.

Before I left, I also bought a Google phone. It was like a little computer: You could go on the Internet with it, but it was a little more expensive than a normal cell phone. They said it would work with any Wi-Fi, and there were Wi-Fi hotspots everywhere you went, all over the place in Portland, and I was told it was the same in Europe. I had signed up on a couch-surfing website, and I would need to be on the Internet, so it would end up saving me money on Internet cafés. I didn't have my own computer, so I felt like the phone was an investment. I paid extra at T-Mobile for a "European package" on the Google phone, to make sure it would work while I was traveling.

I told the nursing agency I'd probably be gone around three weeks, maybe just two, or a little closer to four. They said it was fine, to just give them a call or an email when I wanted them to book me again. That's a great thing about agency work: You're a little freer.

I worked as many shifts as I could get, up to the day before I left Portland, to make sure I'd have enough money. I knew my last paycheck would get put straight onto my prepaid credit card. I calculated that would bring the balance up to about $1,200, which I figured would be enough to buy the plane ticket back to Portland and maybe take a side trip to Paris too.

I knew I'd probably be coming back to Portland low on cash, so I paid Chloe the rent for November and December before I left, and I filled up the tank of my Jeep with gas. That way, I figured, when I got back at least I'd have a full gas tank and the rent would be OK, so I'd be able to make it till my next paycheck was put on my card.

When I got on the plane at Portland International Airport, they actually bumped me up! They said they had a window seat in first class, and asked if I would I like it. I said, "Yeah, sure I'd like it." I was thinking, *Wow, this was really meant to be, like it was a sign, this is going to be a good trip.*

I guess it was, all things considered, in a weird kind of way. I wanted to experience different cultures; that was my original goal and, boy, did I do that, way beyond my expectations.

⚜ ⚜ ⚜

The plane ride was rough. It was a Lufthansa flight, and we were going all the way from Portland to Frankfurt, Germany, no stops. It was really turbulent over the ocean. It had been a long time since I'd flown anywhere, and I had to take some Dramamine, but I had all that stuff in a medical kit in my bag.

I thought I was prepared for everything. I even had some canned food with me. Maureen had traveled all over, and she said you should bring nonperishable items just in case you're in a bind. It was a good way to save some money, because eating at restaurants all the time can get pretty expensive.

While I was on the plane, my Google phone quit working. I figured that was normal since we were in the air, but the camera continued to work, so I took some pictures of the sky out of the window before it got dark. It reminded me of a conversation Chloe and I had had one time. I asked her, "In your next lifetime, if you could come back in any form, which one would you choose, what would you be?"

She said, almost without hesitation, "An eagle! Then I would be free to go wherever I want. I could fly anywhere!"

Then she asked me what I'd pick, and I chose a caterpillar. It was the biggest transformation I could think of. A caterpillar starts out as a larva and becomes a beautiful butterfly and flies away, and I used to love watching butterflies when I was a kid working in my parents' garden.

The photo I took was beautiful, blue sky as far as you could see and down below were snow-topped mountains. I was going to give it to Chloe when I got back home and tell her this was her eagle view.

⚜ ⚜ ⚜

I had a couple of hours at the Frankfurt airport before my flight to Madrid, so I checked my Google phone again. It still didn't work. There was a phone store at the Frankfurt airport, and the guy spoke some English, but he just cracked up laughing when I told him the problem.

He said, "No American phones work over here."

I said, "No, you don't understand, I bought the European package," and then he really started laughing, and said, "Yeah, they got you too, they all do it."

I didn't know whether to take him seriously. There's a T-Mobile company in Germany, they even had ads up in the airport, and I tried really hard to get a hold of them while I was waiting for my flight. There was this guy sitting beside me—he was German but he spoke English, and his phone was T-Mobile. I finally asked him, and he let me use his phone to call the German T-Mobile. I figured that way we could work it out.

The customer-service people spoke a little English, but they said if I bought service in America, they didn't have me in their records. They said, "Ohhh, that's a *different* T-Mobile. Sorry, there's nothing we can do for you here, we're not connected at all to that T-Mobile, we can't even pull up your account, we have nothing to do with each other."

I thought, *Uh-oh, no phone, no email, and no couch-surfing.* I was really counting on the couch-surfing so I could keep within my budget. But I figured maybe the phone would just start working when I got to Spain, and if it didn't, I could just go to an Internet café and work it out with T-Mobile in America, because it had to mean something, paying extra for a European package.

⚜ ⚜ ⚜

Before I left Portland, I asked people I knew who had been to Spain about getting around once I got over there, and they all said the same thing: They have trains to take you everywhere. I think they called it the Eurorail. I asked if I should try to buy tickets before I left and they all said the same thing again: It's cheaper just to buy the tickets once you're over there.

But it was later than I thought it would be when I got to Madrid, because of the time change and everything, and it turned out there is no train from Madrid to Marbella. There's a bus, but it was too late to buy a ticket to the condo, so I needed to spend the night in Madrid at a hostel or hotel.

I asked at the tourist desk in the airport for some help with that. They didn't want to speak English ("This is Spain, you know, Spanish"), but they gave me a list of hostels and hotels and told me where to get off the subway.

So I got onto the subway with my big suitcase and backpack. The subway in Madrid is really intense; there's nothing like it anywhere I've ever lived before. In Portland, there's the Max train, but it's aboveground, with one tunnel by the zoo, so I'd never seen a real subway before. On the Max, you can read the stops as you approach them. But in Spain, they just announce them over a loud-speaker, and of course it's in Spanish. I know a little Spanish, but they were talking so fast on the loudspeaker, I couldn't understand what they were saying.

I was a little overwhelmed at first, and I got lost transferring at a station way underground. None of the escalators or elevators worked, and there were no signs anywhere. It made me think about the train bombings in Madrid a couple of years ago, and the subway bombings in London. I met this couple from Australia, who were also lost, and they had some big suitcases. All these people were swarming past us as we struggled to pull our luggage up the stairs, and none of them offered to help.

We made it out finally, and the Australian couple asked where I was staying. I explained about the list, and they suggested I try at their hostel. The room was forty-nine euro, and the elevator was a little creepy, but the building was beautiful, with a marble staircase and wood floors, so I spent the night there.

The next morning I found the bus station and bought a ticket. The bus ride was a lot longer than I thought it was going to be, eight or nine hours, and it was cheaper if you traveled at night. So I found an Internet café and emailed the people from the condo to let them know I would be a day late. They emailed me right back and were very nice about it. They said they'd leave the key in an envelope with the guard at the gate. I also emailed T-Mobile, told them I was having trouble getting the phone to work, and asked them to get back to me as soon as possible. Everything seemed like it was going fine.

When the bus arrived in Marbella the next morning, I decided to take a cab to the condo, so I wouldn't have trouble finding the place. That's what Maureen suggested I should do. The driver said it was fourteen euros. The manager from the condo told me the next day it really should only cost nine euros to make the trip, but it's a good thing I did take a cab, because the driver was really helpful, so that was OK.

See, I've never been out of America, so I'm used to American locks. They're quite simple: You put the key in, turn the knob, and push the door open. There was a gate with a lock to get into the condo, and the door had two more locks, and for all of them you had to turn the key *three* times to the right or left, depending on which lock it was.

Luckily the taxi driver followed me in to see if I was OK, and he took the key and showed me, see, three times this way or that way. *Boy*, I thought, *even doors and locks are different here.*

It was a really nice condo in a modern development, two-story Spanish-style buildings and a pool, but it was the end of fall, so the pool was closed and a lot of the condos were empty. I had never seen shutters like the ones they had on these windows and doors.

They were like metal curtains that rolled down and shut off all the light. Once everything was all closed up, it felt like I was in a virus lab or something, completely sealed off from the world outside. It was a weird feeling.

I wondered why there were so many locks, and what the shutters were supposed to keep out. I hoped it was only the weather, but I also thought there must be a lot of crime around here.

The condo was walking distance to the beach. I went down there every day that was free, of course, and when it was clear, I could see the Rock of Gibraltar, which was really cool.

I had some bad experiences with some of the people in Marbella. It's a ritzy kind of town, with palm trees and lots of big new buildings, and everything is real expensive, especially restaurants, so I went to the grocery store, bought stuff, and cooked at the condo. I didn't stay out late; from all the locks and shutters everywhere, I got the feeling it might not be safe.

I guess there are lots of tourists in Marbella, but it wasn't tourist season, and the people aren't real fond of Americans, especially if you don't speak fluent Spanish and you're not spending lots of cash. Things were really bad with the economy, and people talked about it like it was our fault, or my fault, because I'm from America. I'd be asking directions at a shop or just from a passerby, and they'd ask where I was from, and when I said, "America," they'd just put their hands up and back away. A couple of people said, "Thanks for the economy." One man said, "I have no retirement because of you," and he spat; he actually spat on the ground beside my boots.

Of course, in America most people don't spit on the ground because it's considered bad manners. I would soon realize this is a common practice in Europe.

So, it was pretty negative energy in Spain. I guess I didn't expect people to be so judgmental just because of the country I was born in, like I was a symbol of the American political system. I'd been told, "Oh, they'll love you in Spain, they love the blonde-haired women, you'll have a great time. It's in France you'll have to watch out. In France nobody has time to give you directions, and if you don't speak French you may have trouble getting around."

I didn't plan on staying long, so it wasn't a big deal, but if this was Spain, I really didn't know what to expect if I did make it to France.

⚜ ⚜ ⚜

I ended up spending a lot of time in the condo and at the beach reading. I was paying all this money to see Europe, and it might be the only time in my life I would ever go. But I just didn't get a good feeling walking around Marbella, and I knew there were other ways I could use the time, like meditating and walking on the beach.

I had brought some books with me, mostly by Eckhart Tolle, who is often considered a disciple of the philosopher and spiritual master J. Krishnamurti. They were books I wanted to read again and think about. I guess I first read *The Power of Now* in August or September. I'd been talking with Alex, a Chilean CMA I used to work with quite a bit. He was a very kind person, and the first time we met it was at a group home. There were some very disturbed teenagers, and the people who worked there could be tough to work with. They seldom helped the agency staff out. Often if you're agency staff, the regular nurses will give you extra work to do while they sit around and watch TV. However, you can't complain: It's the deal because you're agency. Alex, who I'd never met, was just coming off graveyard shift. While I was washing dishes in the kitchen, he went upstairs and totally cleaned a bedroom, changed the linens, and did a lot of the work that I was supposed to do.

Working agency, when you meet someone who's nice to you, it sticks in your head, so I was always glad to see Alex. Plus, at the time I had some friends from Mexico and I was going through a phase of trying to learn Spanish. He said he'd help me, so he was just a sincerely nice guy.

We both started to work a lot at an assisted-living facility, Irvington Village, near Martin Luther King Blvd, in Portland. There are about a hundred rooms, and some of the people have Alzheimer's or physical disabilities; they take a lot of medications or they need some type of assistance. The work can be hard. But Irvington is one of the few places where once your job is done, nobody minds if you sit down and drink a cup of coffee and maybe talk for a little while, so we got to talking.

Alex used to tell me, "We're all the same." He'd say that in almost every conversation, and I really didn't get what he meant. Finally he said it again one evening, and I asked, "Do you mean like the equation for mass energy equivalence, $E=mc^2$? We're all energy, and energy broken down to matter is all the same, is that what you mean?"

Alex smiled. He said, "Yes, but it's more than that. We're all connected, you just have to learn how to see and feel it."

Another night at Irvington Village we were talking about perception, and Alex said, "Do you like to fish, have you ever gone fishing?"

I said, "Yeah, I used to eat a lot of crawfish and fresh seafood in Louisiana."

Alex continued, "So you catch the fish, you go home, cook it, and you eat it. Do you feel sad?"

I said, "No, I feel full."

"OK," he said, "but somebody buys you a fish, you bring it home and put it in a fish tank, name it John and give it a birth certificate, and it dies the next day. You feel sad then, right?"

I said, "Yes, I probably would."

He said, "The only difference was your perception of each fish. That's what made you feel sad."

The next day I went to a bookstore, and I picked up four books: One new-age self-help and a couple of science books. I like to read something I can learn from, like virology or physics. I went and got some coffee at the Starbucks inside the store and sat down with the books. I was only going to buy one, so I needed to figure out which. I opened up the new-age book, just randomly in the middle, and right there on that page was the story about the fish named John, with the birth certificate. Alex never told me there was a *book*.

So that's the book I bought. It was *The Power of Now* by Eckhart Tolle. Parts of it really made sense to me right away. I really took in the whole idea that we're all caught up in time. It seemed like all I ever really thought about was stuff that had already happened, or things that might happen in the future, one day, if. It was all just ruminating, turning little scenarios in my head over and over, and I was beginning to realize that Eckhart Tolle was right: It meant I was never really present in my life right now.

I had trouble understanding a lot of the book, though. One day a nurse I worked with saw *The Power of Now* in my bag and she asked, "How you doing with that?" She said there was another book by Eckhart Tolle I should read first, that it was a lot easier to understand and better to start with.

So then I bought *A New Earth,* and it was good, really wise, and much easier for me to understand. It made me much more aware of how attached I was to stuff and how much unease and worry I was generating from just wanting more.

I started to realize how much I identified with my clothes, my DVD collection, and my little Daihatsu Jeep; I started doing some yoga and meditating again. It was something I did when I was younger: get still, focus on each breath, and gradually try to go beyond thought, start becoming aware of when you're thinking and feel the gaps, the spaces between thoughts. I was learning that I needed to realize my life situation was not my life. I was trying to feel the aliveness inside my body, the life energy, instead of just feeling like it was a heavy load I had to haul around. I tried to stop blaming and complaining.

I also got rid of a bunch of personal possessions. I felt I had been attaching myself to *stuff* instead of opening up to just *being.* I realized how much emotional baggage I was carrying around from my past, and I tried to shake some of it off and learn how to surrender to the present moment. This is my life, right here, right now.

I guess reading Eckhart Tolle made me a lot more patient with other people. I had less irritation and bitterness inside me than before. I was able to really start letting go of a lot of pain and sadness I was carrying around from things that had happened in the past. If someone said something that annoyed me, I could at least recognize what I was doing, and say to myself, wait a minute, this isn't a big deal, what's the irritation about? Then I'd calm down, shift perspective, and try to put myself in their shoes.

So, while I was in Spain I did a lot of soul searching and meditating, and I went to the beach every day. The people there just weren't what I expected. They were judging me because of the country I was born in instead of realizing we're all people; regardless of which part of the planet we're born on, we're all the same. So, it wasn't the vacation I'd had in mind.

But I realized, I *was* born in America, and even if I didn't ever vote for George W. Bush, America *was* somewhat responsible for a lot of damage to the world economy. So I tried to put myself in their shoes. I thought, *I can learn from this, I can grow from this, I can use this.*

⚜ ⚜ ⚜

When the two weeks were over at the condo, I still hadn't received a single response from T-Mobile. I emailed them repeatedly but they just never emailed back. So I still had no service on my Google phone, and that meant I probably wasn't going to get much couch-surfing off the ground, but someone told me they have Wi-Fi everywhere in Paris and they should be able to fix it there.

I still hadn't touched the money on my prepaid credit card, because I was keeping that for my return flight. I was running a little low on cash, but I was being really careful with my money in Marbella, because I wanted so much to go to France, even if it was just for a couple of days. France sounds so exotic, and I was that close. I wanted to see Paris just once in my life. I honestly felt like if I didn't go then, it might never happen.

So I took a bus to Valencia and another bus to Barcelona, and then I was planning to take the night express train to Paris. Barcelona's really pretty and I had a few hours waiting on the train, so I walked around the city. What a terrific place! I did like some things about Spain. Barcelona seemed like a very open-minded kind of city—right in front of the train station, I saw a man riding a bicycle stark naked!

It reminded me of the woman in Portland who's famous for riding her bike around in the nude. That's not something you'll see in most parts of the United States, and it was one reason I liked Portland. The people might seem reserved, they don't greet each other with a hug and kiss like in Louisiana, and they're a little funny about their "own personal space," but in Portland they're also very liberal and easygoing.

There was a mix-up with my train ticket in Barcelona. The woman put me on a train for the next day even though I wanted to travel overnight and save on the hotel bills, and I didn't have enough money for any extras, so I had to point it out. She was nice, and so embarrassed about it that she upgraded me to a sleeper, which was great. There were four bunk beds in a little bitty compartment with three other women, and they all spoke a little English.

The train was really cool too. I'd never been on a big train like that, and it went so fast, it was like a roller coaster. I'd feel the train swooping around the bends all night and kind of lose my stomach. At first I was scared that I'd fall out of the bunk bed or that we were going to crash, but then I remembered what Eckhart Tolle says: I was resisting. This was a new experience and I was resisting it. When I let myself relax and stopped resisting, I started to enjoy it and I realized it wasn't scary; it was more like a ride at Disney World.

Two of the women I was sharing the compartment with, Maria Paulina and Christabelle, were from Brazil, and when we got off the train in Paris the next morning, they suggested I come back to their hostel and get a room there. We were all struggling in the metro. They had a lot of luggage, and the Paris subway has a lot of stairs too. A man came up and asked, "Do you need some help?" He wasn't trying anything on us, he was just being nice. So, straightaway the vibe was different in France, and it wasn't what I'd expected; people were really helpful.

The Brazilian girls were staying at Pont Marie. It was a hostel, like a hotel for backpackers, but it was a really nice building, and it was sixty euros a night, much more than I'd expected. The guy at the desk said if we all three shared a room it would be cheaper, so we decided to do that. It was early in the morning, so after we checked in and washed up, we went right out.

Our first priority was an Internet café, because Paulina's purse had been stolen in Spain and she needed to check that all her cards and stuff had been canceled, and I wanted to book my plane out. It didn't look like I'd get to London on this trip, and I wasn't planning to stay more than two or three nights in Paris, with the hostel being so pricey. There wasn't much hope I could get the Google phone to work and it looked like I was going to run out of money pretty quickly, so I needed to be sure I had my reservation to go back home.

We found an Internet café on Boulevard de Sébastopol, near the Louvre. I checked my email and I still didn't have any answer from T-Mobile. The plane tickets were a bit more expensive than they had been on the way over, and that surprised me, but I got one booked for Monday for a little less than $700.

This was Friday, and I figured it would take at least a day to transfer the payment from my prepaid credit card, so I could relax and see Paris over the weekend.

The weather was beautiful, crisp and clear, and the sun was shining, so we walked down rue de Rivoli to the Louvre. The Brazilian girls were showing me around—they'd been to Paris before.

"This is the main street," Paulina said. "Pretty much everything is around here, if you know where this street is, you're not lost."

⚜ ⚜ ⚜

Paris was beautiful, the buildings and the people too, and the boots. Everyone wore the most elegant boots and shoes. The women didn't seem to wear much makeup, but they had high cheekbones and they knew how to make themselves look pretty, and people were friendly: If you asked directions, they would try to help you.

I loved the Louvre right away, and walking around the outside of the museum, it has a very peaceful presence. The first time I went there, we walked in from the big doorway at the eastern end, and it looked like it was locked, but on either side are two smaller doors that are open. You enter through an archway with sixteen graceful columns. They're so beautiful.

At the end of this archway you're expecting to be inside a building, but surprise, it's a grand illusion: There's no ceiling, you're still outside. You're surrounded by beautiful buildings on all sides, and there are statues embedded in the walls like they're just beginning to grow out of them. It's a great feeling of surprise, peace, and joy.

⚜ ⚜ ⚜

When we looked through the far doorway, we caught a glimpse of the real heart of the Louvre, the glass pyramids. Around them stretched two long stone buildings like grand arms, which I knew were full of art and peace.

That first day, we hung out at the Louvre for a little bit and took pictures, and then we went our separate ways. I was walking down past the Louvre, along Rivoli, when I saw the Eiffel Tower from behind a building. It seemed so close, I just had to see it.

So, I walked there. It's over a mile, but I didn't realize that at first. By the time I walked all the way to it, the sun was going down. I remember, I was walking down a little side street and I knew I was getting closer to it, but all the old apartment buildings were crowded in high enough that they masked the sky. I turned a corner and *boom*, there was the Eiffel Tower. It was huge and right above me. Then, just like someone flicked a switch, the lights went on, strong lines of light all up and down it, and they began to shimmer and twinkle, like a web of tiny stars.

It was awesome.

I stayed for a while, and I wanted to go up the tower, but I didn't want to spend the money for a ticket. Still, seeing it that way was special.

⚜ ⚜ ⚜

The Brazilian women were planning to leave early the next day and take a train down to the south of France.

I didn't have anywhere else to go, so I told the guy downstairs I'd pay for another night at the hostel. Only this time I was by myself, so of course it was going to cost more and I was kind of worried about that.

The next morning the Brazilian girls left before sunrise, and when I went downstairs, there was a big commotion in the breakfast room. Everyone was talking about Air France going on strike, and I couldn't remember which airline my ticket was with, so I went back to the Internet café to check my email. And sure enough, there was an email that said the airline was on strike, and if you hadn't bought insurance you might have lost your ticket.

There was a contact address that you could email questions, so I did, and the agency said if you didn't pay the insurance, they didn't have to guarantee your flight.

See, I'd looked into insurance before I left. I asked several people I knew had been to Europe, and they all said, "Stop worrying. Don't buy the insurance. It's just a way for the airline or agency to get more money from you. Everything's going to be fine."

But it wasn't fine. I wasn't in a great situation, but it wasn't life or death. I was upset, but I just assumed if they had taken the money for the flight, they would reimburse it. I figured I had lost this flight home, so I would just have to book another one. I was sure there was enough money left on the prepaid credit card to pay for it.

I tried to check the balance on my prepaid credit card, but the website just kept coming up unavailable, so I started looking at different travel agency websites in the Internet café. At first I went to Orbitz.com, the website where had I originally booked my flight, and I saw that tickets were over $1,000. My heart sank, but when you get on that kind of website, all these little pop-up ads from competitors start coming in like crazy—you click on one and two more come in.

I started clicking on the ones that said CHEAP FLIGHT, but all the flights were over $1,000 everywhere I looked, and as I kept clicking, the prices seemed to be heading upwards.

I found a ticket for a little over $800 that was leaving Friday, and I went ahead and booked that one. I knew it would take at least a day to clear payment, and I figured the strike would probably end quickly. I thought if I could just make it for a few days, the price would come down after the strike ended and then I'd be fine. But again, I didn't buy insurance, because I was afraid I didn't have enough to cover that. I knew I was cutting it close.

Then I walked back down Rivoli to see the Louvre again. I wanted to go inside and look at the paintings, but the ticket to get in was nine euros. I was running low on cash, so I window-shopped and walked around the river, then went back to the Eiffel Tower to see the lights again, and I fed the pigeons some of the sandwich I bought for lunch.

⚜ ⚜ ⚜

The next day I had almost no cash left, so I checked out of the hostel, but I asked if I could leave my luggage in their storage room. I explained that my plane ticket was messed up because of the strike, and I was trying to get everything straightened out, so could I please leave my stuff with them for a while. They were pretty nice about it, and said with Air France being out of commission, I wasn't the only person having trouble working things out.

I looked all day for a hostel or a hotel that would be cheaper, but I guess I wasn't looking in the right neighborhoods because they all seemed to be so expensive. Finally, when it was getting late, I gave in and paid seventy euros for the night at a hotel. The hostel would have been a little cheaper, but it was way across town and I was exhausted. I didn't want to use the prepaid credit card, but I figured I had to, because I didn't have enough cash left to cover it.

I stayed up late thinking about it, and couldn't sleep much. I was sure I had the plane ticket all sewed up for Friday morning, but that still meant another four nights in Paris. I didn't know how much money was left on the prepaid credit card, but I was afraid I was cutting it close, and if I spent another night in a hotel or hostel and put that on the card too, maybe I wouldn't be able to make the payment for the flight home.

I didn't realize at that moment that they added on hundreds of dollars in airport fees and taxes, and there never was $1,200 on that prepaid credit card, either.

I don't know exactly what had happened; maybe I miscalculated taxes, or maybe the nursing agency messed up the payroll calculations on my last paycheck—it was a new system and it had happened before—or maybe it didn't get transferred correctly. Perhaps T-Mobile took more off my card than they said they would. It could have been the health club; I told them I was canceling my membership, but sometimes they kind of forgot and kept taking their dues.

Any one of those things could have been enough to throw it off, and I'm not sure which one it was, but in reality there was very little money left on the card.

If I had known that at the time, I'd have really panicked, because I just didn't have enough money left to get back home to America.

2

A Dark New World

I guess it was about ten at night, and I was riding the subway. It was really cold and I knew it wasn't going to run all night long, but I didn't have any kind of plan. I was starting to realize what a jam I was in. I had about thirty-five euros in my pocket, and I told myself I couldn't use the prepaid card, because I was still waiting for the ticket payment to go through, so that meant I didn't have enough money for a place to stay.

The tears started leaking out as I sat there on the train. I was on line 6. It goes aboveground a lot, an d I like it better when the train's running aboveground. The metro train came out into the night air, and boom, there was the Eiffel Tower right beside me, huge and all lit up.

It was the strangest feeling. I was so lost, and it was so big and close. I felt like I could just reach out and touch it. It was like a message that brought me back to the present moment.

Later that night, I was on the street near the Louvre looking at my metro map. Even though it was a subway map, I used it to figure out my way around town because it had the major landmarks on it. A guy came up and offered to buy me a cup of coffee. This was before I realized how you have to avoid men in Paris at night, but I kept saying, "No, sorry, gotta go here, gotta go there," and he asked where I was staying.

I said I was still working on that, and he looked at me kind of knowingly; maybe he was homeless or had been at one time. He is the first one that told me this: "If you don't have a place to stay, you have to walk. You have to keep moving. It's not safe for a woman alone in Paris at night."

So that's what put the idea in my head: I would just walk. I didn't think I could actually walk all night, but walking keeps you warm, and now I figured it could keep me safe.

I did try to stop walking a few times, but if you're a woman, it seems like someone is always trying to grab you or follow you or bother you in some way if you sit down for too long, especially if you're blond—and once they learn you speak English, they're so persistent. They won't leave you alone.

All night I walked from the Louvre to the Eiffel Tower, and then I started circling around there. I felt safer, or at least halfway safer, around the military police in camouflage outfits with their big guns. You don't see them there all the time, but you figure they're always somewhere around.

And the lights of the Eiffel Tower were on until one in the morning. It's a funny thing about buildings—sometimes they really have a presence. The Eiffel Tower reminded me of a huge fairy godmother; it was beautiful, and every hour it shimmered in the sky. In the fog, the top of it was just a cloud of light, like a beacon reminding me to ground myself.

But it was really cold that night, and I wasn't prepared to stay out in the weather. I just had a thin knee-length coat and a sweater on. My suitcase was still at the hostel, so I only had my backpack and a plastic bag with me, but they were getting heavy.

If you stay close to the buildings, there's some warmth that seeps out of them, but at 1:00 AM when the lights go out, the Eiffel Tower is not so reassuring anymore. It kind of looms over you, a big hunk of dark metal, fierce and scary, and there's a bitter wind coming off the river.

Then I walked from the Eiffel Tower back to the Louvre. I knew that route and I felt safer around those two places, and when I got to the Louvre, I knew that was the right place to be. The old Louvre courtyard is closed at night, but the pyramids and the long arms that stretched into the garden are open. You can go there all night long.

The lights are always on, and there's the large dim light of the glass pyramid, which glows like a big night-light, solemn, deep and calm. The buildings are dark, but the statues that run along all the sides of the buildings on the first floor are lit until late. A big one on the rooftop looks kind of like a watchful angel, and there's a stone bench you can sit on that's built into the wall, angled just right so it feels like he's looking down straight at you.

Plus there are the military police in camouflage outfits and berets doing rounds from time to time, so I felt a little more protected.

It was late at night, but there were still people walking around, regular people out on dates or maybe tourists. And there are a lot of hotels around the Louvre that keep their lights on all night, like there's someone staying up in the office. I guess I figured if I screamed, someone might hear me, and even if it wasn't his or her job, he or she might help out.

You walk all night. Anyone can do it. You're tired, but it's not safe to stop for long. Bad people hang out around the Louvre at night—actually, it seems like bad people hang out everywhere in Paris at night. I would just sit on a bench, even one out in the open near the pyramid where it was lit, and men would come out of nowhere, like they were hiding in a shadow, and sit next to me and try to touch me or put their arm around me.

They could be persistent. One guy made gestures with his hands like he wanted me to do something sexual to him, then he kept taking my hand and trying to put it on his crotch. He was very hard to shake.

Everything's fine when the guards are around, but never at times like that, when the wolves come out. Luckily most of them may follow you for a bit, but once they realize you're serious and you want to be far away from them, they'll eventually drop it, and you can just walk away.

A couple of times I sat on benches for maybe ten or fifteen minutes. It was too cold to sit still for long. I walked up and down by the river, where there are statues of lions with cherubs on each side. One is putting a flower necklace on a lion and the other one is fanning him with a huge feather. Somehow they made me feel safer, like they were friendly lions, sitting on top of their pedestals, guarding against danger.

And then I walked along Rivoli. As long as I knew where rue de Rivoli was, I knew I wouldn't get lost. I remember about five in the morning, I found a tangerine on the ground and thought, *Oh, breakfast,* and ate it.

They have these magic toilets that sit on the pavement in Paris, like little rooms you can walk into, for free. You just push the button and the door opens. Some of them are closed from 11:00 PM to 6:00 AM, but a few are open 24/7. You can use the toilet and wash your hands. There's a little sink-hole in the wall where the water runs down, even though it's ice cold in the winter. When you walk out, the floor has some kind of pressure sensor that feels your weight lift, so the whole room is supposed to clean itself and wait for the next person to come in.

Most of them are heated, and once you get inside, the door will stay closed for fifteen minutes if you don't manually open it. Even if you don't need to use the toilet, fifteen minutes of warmth is a welcome break when you're freezing. You just have to get past the smell. I actually saw a couple of magic toilets that had a pole or umbrella jammed in the pressure weight so the door wouldn't open automatically: There were people living in the magic toilets!

It's very enlightening to have to rely on something like those toilets, and they're very humbling, because most of them don't work. They're filthy, they reek, they typically don't have toilet paper, the water in the sink usually doesn't run, and there's never a toilet seat on the toilet. At first I was really quite shocked. I remember thinking, *What's up with that?* Then I tried to see it from a different perspective. Maybe I'm just a lazy American who's used to the luxury of sitting down on a nice plastic toilet seat.

The most useless thing I brought with me from America was a travel-size package of Charmin toilet-seat covers. It makes me laugh when I think of them now. I really didn't have any idea what to expect on this trip.

If you don't have money to go to a café, this is the toilet you're going to use, because it's free. In a lot of ways, you're lucky to have it. We didn't have anything like that in Oregon, so I felt humbled and grateful. Like I said, the magic toilets in Paris are very enlightening.

⚜ ⚜ ⚜

So that was my first night on the street. When it was morning, I went to McDonald's. In America they have sausage or egg and cheese biscuits for ninety-nine cents; I was hungry and thought it would be a cheap breakfast. When I got there, I realized they don't have anything cheap on the menu for breakfast at McDonald's in Paris, so I came back a little later, when they started serving hamburgers. They're only ninety-five cents.

Then I went back to the Internet café. I guess Air France was still on strike. I tried to access the balance on my prepaid credit card again, but it just kept coming up unavailable, like the website wasn't working. I checked the price of plane tickets, and I couldn't believe they were going up even higher. I remember telling myself, don't panic, all you have to do is make it for three more nights till your flight home.

My Google phone still wasn't working, so I bought a phone card to call Chloe. I wanted to tell her I was stuck and when I'd actually be coming back, plus it would have been comforting just to hear her voice.

But I couldn't get the phone card to work, so I called the operator from a phone booth, but she said they don't make operator calls to the United States anymore; that service had been discontinued.

I just wasn't prepared for this stuff. I'd never been out of America, and I guess I was pretty naive in terms of things working so differently in other parts of the world. I just took it for granted that everything would be similar to what I knew, until suddenly it wasn't. But I tried to keep a positive perspective. I kept telling myself, be logical, they're not going to stay on strike forever and the ticket prices have to come down, it's all going to be OK. You only have to make it for a few days, then you'll be fine.

⚜ ⚜ ⚜

I spent a lot of time sitting on benches that day, and then it was my second night on the street: time to start walking again. Around midnight, I remember standing by the water close to the Eiffel Tower. My body was aching and I was exhausted both mentally and physically, so I stopped to take a quick rest on a bench.

People were walking past like it was daylight—this is Paris, I guess a lot of people stay out late. Several men stopped to talk to me, more wolves, but they weren't as aggressive that night as they sometimes were. I just walked down the path to a different bench to discourage them, and then I'd go across the street to a bench there, then back up and down and across the street again, so I could rest a few minutes.

They almost always offer to buy you a drink, and when you refuse, they offer you café. There were many times I was cold and a warm cup of coffee would have felt good, but after that one guy offered to buy me café my first night on the street, I learned they can be hard to shake.

I couldn't walk anymore. My feet were swollen up past the ankles, and there was a constant dull, moderate ache and then waves of knife-stabbing pain. I have sciatica pain in both hips, a bee-stinging pain that starts in my upper hip and shoots down my leg to my knees, but I also have plantar fasciitis, which is worse.

The whole ligament along the sole of my foot gets inflamed, and after a few years I also developed fibroid tumors on the ligament. It feels like you're walking with pebbles stuck inside your boot under the arch of your foot, but you can't empty them out because they're attached to your ligament. This problem started after working years as a nursing assistant, on my feet all the time.

A doctor in Portland once told me if it kept getting worse I might need to have an operation, but with no health insurance, I couldn't even afford the money for the MRI he said I needed. So I just ended up buying a pair of orthopedic boots from Z-CoiL. They aren't pretty, but they have springs in the heel that help absorb the impact of each step.

Now, even with the Z-CoiL boots, I couldn't take the pain of walking any longer. I sat on a bench beside some bushes along the river near the Eiffel Tower, wishing I could just become invisible, longing for a place to hide, a place to sleep. Then I saw some rats dart out of the bushes beside me.

I had a pet rat once. I worked as a lab assistant for a while in college and befriended this rat, but after the test period was over, they told me to take her over to the euthanasia room and put her in the tank. I just couldn't, and my supervisor said, "Do it or take her home with you," so I took her home. She was one of the best pets I ever had: litter-box trained and she'd come when I called her.

Rats are survivors, and they're very intelligent problem solvers. These Paris rats were big, dark, and sleek. They looked kind of beautiful. They were scurrying in and out of the bushes, some in pairs and some alone. I guessed there was a nest—it was a fairly thick clump of bushes.

I bent down to take a closer look, and I thought there could be room to crawl up underneath the branches. It looked like a good space; somewhere I could curl up and hide, and maybe sleep a little, much safer than out in the open with the wolves.

I crawled on my knees under the branches, and saw what looked like a little nest of twigs and leaves. The soil had a strong odor, and it reminded me of the vegetable garden I planted with Chloe. The ground was very cold, hard, and wet, so I needed to insulate it with something if I was going to lie down.

I stood up and looked around, and down a little incline, on the sidewalk, there were piles of leaves under the street lamps. I wasn't really thinking anymore—it was like the gears had shifted to survival mode. I walked over, took off my knee-length coat, laid it on the ground, and piled as many leaves onto it as I could.

They were damp, and I pulled the corners of the coat together, dragged it up the incline to the bushes, and emptied out the leaves. It wasn't nearly enough for a bed, so I did it again and again till I could barely stand. Then I crawled up under the bushes and brushed the leaves up against and under me, and covered myself from head to toe with them as I lay down.

The rats came over after a little while, to check me out. They seemed to realize I didn't mean them any harm, and I knew they didn't mean me any. They just sniffed at me, and then they found my plastic bag, which had a small piece of bread inside. They crawled into the bag and dragged it out with them. It made me smile. I figured it was pretty cheap rent for such a safe hiding place.

I felt a sharp puncture in my thigh, like I had lain down on a long thorn. The next day I realized I'd been bitten, not by the rats,

but by some kind of insect or spider. It was red, swollen, and painful, but not nearly as bad as my feet and hips. I halfway forgot
about it after a while.

❖ ❖ ❖

I guess I slept for a couple of hours. It was about three o'clock
when I woke up, and it was freezing. My whole body was shaking
from the cold. I didn't even think, I just grabbed my backpack and
began to walk.

I walked for the rest of the night, and I started to realize what
a bad jam I was in. I was in a foreign country where I couldn't
understand the language, and I was sleeping under a bush with
rats in November, but it wasn't like I was destitute or homeless.

I tried to be positive. It was just a short-term problem. Everything happens for a reason. Being in a different situation can be
enlightening. It can force you to pull on resources you never even
realized you had.

The ticket prices would come down soon and maybe the night
before my flight I could go out to the airport and sleep there, so it
wasn't permanent. "And this too shall pass." 1 Corinthians 10:12.
That's how I felt.

But I really needed to sleep and eat, so once the ticket reservation went through, maybe I could take a little money off the prepaid credit card. I went back to the Internet café, and as soon as I
logged on, I was bombarded with pop-up ads for plane tickets and
travel agency sites. Before I even checked my email, I took a look
at some of the prices and realized they weren't going down at all.

Then I saw the email from the website where I had bought the
airplane ticket. It said I didn't have enough money left on the prepaid credit card to cover it, so I didn't have a reservation. There
was no flight home.

I felt like all the blood drained from my head, and then a wave of
nausea. My heart was pounding like it was going to burst through
my chest. I tried checking the balance on the card, but the website
still wasn't working. I just sat there staring at the computer screen,
kind of in shock, as I began to realize I wouldn't be going home on
Friday. And then I remembered, I'm paying for this, I have to log off.

I walked out of the Internet café in a daze. I guess I was in shock. I felt frozen, like everything was happening at a distance. It's hard to explain. Before that, I knew I was going to get home, it would all work out, and soon this whole mess would be behind me. But now the rescue was gone and I wasn't going home. I was stranded.

I tried to keep everything in perspective; I kept telling myself, don't panic, just stay calm, everything is going to be OK. The ticket prices will go back down and then you'll get a flight home.

"In the midst of conscious suffering there is already the transmutation. The fire of suffering becomes the light of consciousness."

⚜ ⚜ ⚜

Later that morning, I was on the subway with my feet propped up. I was exhausted, and I put my head against the window and tried to nap a little, but the subway was rough and it stopped every few minutes. I had found some of that gold foil stuff they use to wrap flowers in and I was thinking that would insulate me, so I layered it under my coat. This guy followed me out of the subway tunnel and asked, "Where you sleep?"

I said, "I'm fine," which in French is *ça va*, and just kept walking. But he trotted beside me and said, in more or less broken English, that he knew an association that helped people who don't have anywhere to stay—he made the international sign language for sleep, two hands by your ear. He told me he worked for them, and they could help me find a place to sleep that was safe. He would take me there.

There was no one else, so I decided I had no choice except to trust him. He took me to a place called Agora, which when you get down to it, probably saved my life.

This guy was from Panama, and he had some long, complicated Panamanian name, but he said his mom called him Tico. He was young, dark-skinned, and kind of looked like the actor Cuba Gooding, Jr. He said he also worked as a cook, and he spoke a little broken English. I thought he spoke good French too, but I figured out later, his French was actually very basic. When I started learning some French, I would question how stable Tico was mentally, but

I didn't realize that till a lot later. Not being able to communicate well, it was hard to see it right away.

I believe Tico honestly meant well, though. Agora was on rue des Bourdonnais, pretty close to the Louvre, and there were a lot of homeless people hanging around outside. By far most of them were men, and some of them were kind of rough looking, but that first day nobody bothered me. They just stared.

There was a big, tiled main room with a bunch of Formica tables, and it seemed like you could get coffee for free. All the chairs and tables were crowded and many of the people were laying their head on the tables, trying to sleep.

There was also a glass office, which I realized later is where the social workers sit, because this place Agora was like a day center for homeless people. Tico went into the office and talked to them for a few minutes, and then he came out and said, "None of them speaks English."

"Can't you speak French for me?" I asked, and Tico said we had to make an appointment to come back.

He went back into the office and got a list of what he said were domiciles. I said, "What's a domicile?" and he said it was like a temporary place to live. He said some of these places would let you stay one month, maybe up to three months.

It made me think of Alex back in Oregon. One time he told me how he'd traveled around Europe with a backpack, taking trains and hitchhiking when he ran out of money. He said he spent some time in homeless shelters.

Now that I look back on it, maybe everything really does happen for a reason, like my mom used to say. It meant I knew there were shelters you could get into, so I thought this was worth a try.

As we headed over to the subway, Tico pointed at a building across the road from the Pompidou Centre—which is a big library and museum combined—and he made the international gesture for "shower." I looked at him weirdly, so he showed me: It was a public shower.

You could bathe there for free and it had separate sections for women and men, and people were there on duty, so it looked safe. Actually it looked a little like the showers at a swimming pool, and

I could smell chlorine. There's a pool next door to the showers, but you have to pay for that, so I never went in. The smell reminded me of the swimming pool at the health club I belonged to back in Portland, a familiar smell, like this place was OK.

Then back we went on the subway with the list of domiciles. I'd walked for two days now and had barely slept. My feet, hips, and knees were about done, and in the Paris subway, like Madrid, the stairs seem endless. Perhaps Americans really are lazy. I had never seen so many stairs in my life.

Tico dragged me all over town. He had the list with the addresses and I thought he knew what he was doing and where he was going. When he talked with people, I didn't realize he was barely getting across the basics. Now I do know, because I can speak and understand French a little, but back then I had no idea.

"Oh this one," he'd say, pointing to the list. "This is a good one." And then he'd drag me off to some faraway metro stop. Sometimes he couldn't find the place, so he'd stop people and ask for directions, but they didn't seem to be much help. Other times he found the place, but it was full, sorry, no domiciles available, check back in two weeks.

I don't know what Tico was thinking. A domicile isn't a place to sleep, it's a place to get mail, but at the time, I had no way of knowing that. These offices we were going into were in tall buildings, so I assumed they all had rooms with beds in them somewhere upstairs. Obviously, homeless people need a place to get mail, so they can keep in touch with people, maybe find a job and register for government benefits, if they're eligible for any. But a domicile is just a post-office box.

⚜ ⚜ ⚜

At one point, I couldn't walk anymore. I kept telling Tico I was tired and my feet hurt. I also had a bad cold from being out in the weather, and Tico said he knew a doctor at metro Porte Dauphine, and next thing I knew he was taking me there. It said *Docteur* on the door, so we waited in line with some other people; there was a woman with a scarf around her head like a Muslim, and several other women with children, and a man with gray hair who had a very strong odor and his clothes looked like they needed to be washed.

When it was our turn, Tico showed his ID card and said something in French. The doctor looked at my feet and grimaced. He said my Z-CoiL boots were no good, I should wear sneakers. I tried to explain about arch support, that they were orthopedic boots I paid $250 for and it's not like I could afford another pair. He wrote some prescriptions for inflammation, and for my cold.

We left and Tico said, "This is good," and I explained, "No—no euro, I have no euro for prescriptions." But Tico said, "It's OK, I am the bank."

I needed to use the magic toilet I'd seen about a block back, and while I was gone, Tico walked into a pharmacy and got the drugs the doctor had prescribed. He came out with a plastic bag and handed it to me: There were three boxes of pills and two bottles of cough syrup, lotion, and an ointment for my feet. He said in his broken English that one pill was an antibiotic, one was for inflammation, and the other was for pain.

I was shocked, and I said "No money." But Tico pulled out a green card and waved it around. "Free!" he kept saying.

I was amazed. He had a bag full of medicine, and he was telling me he just walked into a pharmacy, showed his card, and they gave him all this medication for free. In America, even if you have health insurance you have to make a co-payment for each medication— usually about $25 to $50 dollars—so the bag Tico was holding could easily have cost $150 in the United States. I just couldn't believe my eyes.

We walked some more. It was getting late, around eight o'clock, and Tico appeared to be really sorry about the domiciles not working out. He said he'd pay for a room for me tonight. I said "For me only—only me, right?" and he nodded yes and seemed genuinely OK with that. He repeated, "You only."

So, we went back on the metro to Republic, which is a big traffic circle, a little northeast of town, to find a hotel. And actually Tico didn't have enough money, so I had to pay six euros, which was about all I had left in my pocket, but I was so tired it seemed like a small price to pay for a shower and a bed.

I showed my passport and Tico showed his ID, which made me feel a little weird. I didn't want this to be his room, but he was paying for most of it, so I let it go. Then he wanted to come up to the room; he was carrying my backpack, where I put shampoo and some extra clothes. I repeated "No, only me, I stay alone," and he said, "Yes, I carry your bag, then I go."

He'd been carrying it all day so I didn't want to make a big deal about it, but the backpack was pretty heavy and when we unlocked the door he said he was fatigued from the stairs and just sat down on the bed.

I kept asking him to leave, but he wouldn't. He kept saying fatigue. He said, "I stay this side of the bed, promise."

I was really tired and hurting, so I took the medicine and looked at the labels closely. One appeared to be ibuprofen, one was a cough syrup with mostly herbs to clear my sinuses, one was an antibiotic, and the last one looked similar to the Flexeril I took for sciatica pain. I even pulled out the chemical composition and tried to read the precautions, but it was in French. So I took the medicine and lay down. My body didn't seem to be able to do anything else.

The pain medications made me drowsy, and I was just starting to drift off to sleep when Tico put his arm around me. I felt the presence of a wolf—it was the first time I had felt it around him—and without thinking, I jumped up out of the bed.

Tico looked startled by my reaction and he said, "Sorry, no more, is OK." Then about a half hour later, he tried touching me again. He wouldn't stop bothering me, throwing his arm across me. He tried to undo my clothes. I got up and told him to leave, but he wouldn't and he tried to stop me from leaving. At about one thirty, I got out.

I walked from Republic to the Eiffel Tower, to the only halfway safe place I knew: the bush with the rats. It was a long walk through dark streets I didn't know, so I told myself, Paris is like any other city. Stay away from small streets and alleyways, stay on the big roads, and don't go down dark streets when there are no people.

I had a metro map in my pocket, so I kind of knew where I was. I followed the straight lines to Châtelet and then walked down Rivoli to the Louvre. Swing over the river on the footbridge near the big building with a clock on it. That's the Musée d'Orsay, and then it's another two kilometers down the river to the Eiffel Tower. I had a route down already.

I lay down under the bushes for maybe a couple of hours; the leaves were still there. The rats seemed to remember me, and some of them lay next to me like they were keeping me warm. It was freezing, but I didn't feel so alone after they did that; their warm little bodies were very comforting.

I got up when it got too cold to lie on the ground anymore, and then it dawned on me that I'd left my plastic bag in the hotel room. Inside it were my toothbrush and toothpaste and some underwear. I'd left in such a hurry, and I guess I wasn't thinking very sharp after not sleeping for so long. I had to get back to the hotel at Republic before Tico checked out so I could pick it up. I had almost no money left in my pocket for a metro ticket, so I had to walk back.

It was just beginning to be light out when I made it back to Republic. I guess it was probably close to eight o'clock, but the guy at the desk said Tico had already checked out, and he hadn't left anything for me. So now toothbrush, toothpaste, and extra underwear were some more things that I was going to have to manage without.

3

Montesquieu

I walked out of the hotel and thought about what I should do next. I barely had any money left in my pocket. I tried using the prepaid credit card to get money out of the cash machines, but so far at every bank I had tried the card didn't work.

I felt very isolated and alone. The phone card I'd bought was brand-new, but it just wouldn't work. I even asked random people to help me figure it out, but they would try to use it and then hand it back and tell me, "The card's *fini*." (*Fini* is French for "finished.")

And whom would I call? I needed hundreds of dollars, and I didn't know anyone who could spare that kind of money. Most of the people I knew worked two jobs just to pay their bills, and they lived paycheck to paycheck, just like me. Sure, I had some friends, but when everyone works so much, we didn't have a lot of time to develop super-close relationships, so I didn't feel like I could ask them for a loan that big.

Maybe I could have tried to call my father, but I hadn't spoken to him in over ten years, and I didn't think he would help me. I didn't even have his phone number anymore, and it wasn't in my Google phone. I guess I might have called Alex, and I would have said I was stuck in France. Alex would probably have said, "You're not stuck. If you're in France, that's where you are meant to be at this moment in your life. Stop resisting, accept what is."

See, Alex is a man, so his perspective is different. He has traveled all over the world, and lived in twenty-two different countries, and he always said they were some of the best times of his life. One time while he was in Europe, he got in a bind and spent some time in homeless shelters, but that all happened fifteen or twenty years ago. The world was a very different place back then, and I don't think he would have understood how dangerous it is for a woman alone on the streets of Paris.

I had no idea what to do. I just figured it would work out somehow—it had to—and in the meantime, Tico had shown me some resources. There were the free showers, although I didn't need to go there right away, and there was the Agora place near Rivoli where you could get free coffee.

So I walked there, but I got lost, and by the time I arrived, it was too late for coffee. At Agora they only serve coffee at certain times of day, but I got lucky and found a chair to sit down and a place on one of the Formica tables to lay my head.

People came up and started talking to me. Actually, I remember the first day I was in Paris, two or three people came up and asked me what today's day and date was. I thought that was really odd, but now I understood, because when you go so long with no sleep, the days and dates start to run together.

When they closed Agora for lunch, I walked over to the Louvre. It seemed like nobody was going to help me get home, so I walked through the gardens until I felt calm and things began to seem a little more manageable. Sometimes there are people there, feeding pigeons and seagulls. Then I went back and sat on a bench near the café beside the pyramid. It caught the sunlight a little bit, but there was no shelter from the wind.

The Louvre always makes me feel grounded, and I told myself this wasn't the end of the world. I couldn't pay for this ticket, so I'd be stuck in Paris for a while, but I thought the ticket prices would drop. At some point there'd be a ticket I could pay for, so long as I didn't use much of the money on the card. See, I still didn't know how little money was left on my prepaid card, so I told myself it would just be a day or two, and then I'd be fine.

When Agora opened back up again at two in the afternoon, I tried talking to the social workers myself, but nobody there could speak English, and then Tico walked in the door.

I asked him for my plastic bag. He kept saying it was somewhere else. His English wasn't fluent and I had trouble understanding him. He wanted to take me looking for domiciles again, but I said no way. I felt I would be safer on my own. I told him, "You give me the list and I'll figure it out with my metro map."

Finally he did, but it was already afternoon when I set off to find domiciles. I did find a couple: one place wouldn't talk to me, and at the other the guy said they were full, check back in two weeks. I had nowhere else to go, so I went back to Agora.

I ate the last of my canned food that night. It was one of those StarKist premixed tuna salads with a little packet of crackers on the side.

When Agora closed at eight thirty, Tico was still there. He managed to communicate that this time he really would take me somewhere I could sleep, and he promised he wouldn't come in. He said it wasn't far, and it didn't seem like I had many other options.

He took me down Rivoli, to a building on rue Montesquieu. It had tall marble columns like it was once a grand old storefront, but behind them was a rolling metal gate similar to the shutters in Spain. It looked like it was closed up or maybe abandoned, but still, there was a crowd of people waiting outside in the dark, on the sidewalk.

When the building opened up, Tico talked to the guy at the door. Then we went upstairs and Tico went into an office and talked to another man in French, and showed him my passport. When he came out, he told me it was a homeless shelter and I could stay there for one month, maybe more.

What a relief. It didn't matter what the building looked like, it was a place I could lay down and prop my feet up.

I was exhausted, but the guy motioned for me to wait. He showed me a list, like they were expecting other women to come in, and then he pointed upstairs and over at the cots, and shrugged his shoulders, like he wasn't sure where I would sleep. I kept saying it was OK, a cot would be fine, I just needed to lie down, but it wasn't till about eleven thirty that he finally showed me where I was going to sleep.

We went up some more stairs. On the second floor it was just canvas cots laid out in rows, and it was filling up with men, but one floor higher there were actual rooms. They were just for women. When it wasn't too cold and the shelter wasn't too crowded, they tried to keep the women separate from the men at Montesquieu, so they could get a little sleep.

That first time I was lucky. I got to sleep in one of the rooms on the third floor. That didn't happen very often. And I was in a room with just two beds: most rooms have three or four. There was even a heater, and the guy who took me up there showed me a shower down the hallway and gave me a little toothbrush, a small piece of soap, and some toothpaste. No shampoo, but that's OK. You can wash your hair with soap if you have to.

First thing, even though it was already close to midnight, I took a hot shower. The lock on the door was broken, so I put my boots against it. Sure enough, a man came up and pushed the door open while I was in there, and it was the employee who'd shown me around in the first place. Luckily I had just gotten out of the shower, so I was behind the door and pushed it back.

My roommate was an African woman in her thirties. She had a squint and didn't speak much English, so we just kind of nodded and smiled. She seemed kind, but after we lay down, she started itching really frantically. She would get up, scratch like crazy, and shake out the blanket. As she would do this, I could feel the air and dust coming down on me.

I'm a nursing assistant, so I was thinking maybe drugs or scabies. I've seen scabies at nursing homes, and I knew if she had that, then it was probably all over the facility, and I would probably get it too. But I was so exhausted it seemed like it was worth the risk to lie down in a warm bed.

It was hot in the room. The heater was stuck on high and it got really stuffy. My roommate also had a really strong odor, like it had been a long time since she had bathed, so I didn't sleep well. In the morning the whole room smelled, and I wanted to take another shower, but I didn't risk it, because of the door not locking.

There was also no time. When you spend the night at Montesquieu, they wake you up at six thirty in the morning and you're out the door at seven. They turned on the lights and called out something in French, and then it was a big rush of people getting up, getting dressed, and lining up for the toilet. Everyone wanted to be sure they had time to eat a little breakfast before they had to leave.

Downstairs everyone was getting café or hot milk out of very large coffeepots. Then you went over to the counter, where you were handed a small tray with bread, butter, and jam, if there was any. It was all a big rush. At Montesquieu they hustle you out to the street after a few minutes, like they're herding cattle.

At seven, we were all out on the pavement with our stuff, and it was really cold and still dark outside. This whole crowd of people with bags and belongings mostly began shuffling back to Agora, because they open at eight and there's coffee and heat.

With nowhere else to go, I went with them. I had only slept about three hours, since the room was way overheated, my roommate kept getting up and scratching, and I didn't even get to the room till almost midnight. I went to Agora with everyone else and found a table to lay my head on for a while, and tried to nap.

Agora closes for two hours at lunchtime. They clean the place up a bit and I guess the people who work there go to lunch. Tico showed up when it was almost lunchtime. He put his hand to his mouth and said, "Mange," and motioned for me to follow him. I didn't really want to, but I was hungry and broke, so I figured as long as we stayed in public places with people around, it would be OK.

He took me back to the metro, and at first I said, "No, no more metro," remembering the last time he had dragged me around all day. But he motioned with his hands—indicating small—and I was really hungry, so I went with him. He took me way up on line 7, and we walked down a little road to an old one-story building. He talked to the person at the door and motioned for me to come in.

It was like a little cafeteria. I got in line and picked up a tray and they gave me food, a lot of food. It was homeless food; it comes in plastic containers and it's pretty bland and oily, but it was hot and it filled me up. I ate about half and put the other half in my bag for later.

Tico wanted me to go somewhere else with him, but I refused, and said, "No, Agora," so he took me back there on the metro.

At around six that evening people started lining up at the counter where they served café, so I got in line too. When I got up to the counter I asked for café, and they said, "No café," so I sat back down.

I'd eaten lunch, so that was OK, and I knew the shelter on rue Montesquieu would open at nine and there would be a bed for me there. It wasn't a great bed, but it was a whole lot better than the street, and it relieved a lot of my anxiety. I was stuck, it wasn't a great situation with the plane ticket and everything, but I thought if I could just wait, the ticket prices would come down and I'd be fine.

So that night I went back to rue Montesquieu expecting there would be no problem getting in. But the guy at the counter inside the door said no—"No ticket, no stay." He went and got someone who spoke better English, and he said they had told Tico last night that they would let me into Montesquieu for one night, on an emergency basis. But I couldn't stay there again without a special ticket from a social worker or from the emergency hotline for the homeless. They asked for my passport again, and then they started laughing: "American, yeah, you can't stay here."

Finally they did give in, after I pleaded with them. They let me stay another night, but they explained this was really the last time. From now on I had to have a ticket from a social worker or a referral from the help line for the homeless. They said the number was 115. This time there was no bed for me, just one of the canvas camp cots set up on the first floor.

I don't think there were any other women that first night I slept on a cot. It was mostly men, and they wouldn't leave me alone. They put their hands on my leg or my shoulder, and one came up behind me—I was lying on my side—and reached for my crotch. They kept coming over and talking with me, trying to touch me, and I was really getting frightened.

Finally one guy whom I'd seen at Agora, whose name I think was Hakim, stepped in. He didn't speak much English or French, but he was very kind. He was like my self-appointed bodyguard. He motioned to the men to leave me alone, and finally he sat up all night in a chair beside my cot to shoo them away so I could get some sleep. He made the international sleeping sign to me and nodded: go to sleep, it's OK.

⚜ ⚜ ⚜

As soon as they shooed us out of Montesquieu after bread and café, I called 115, the homeless help line, from a phone booth. It was a free call, and I asked if anyone there spoke English and I waited for the right person to come on, and then I told the person my story.

I did this again and again, almost every morning, and sometimes I would hear the operator typing away. I guess they had a file on me, but they needed all the details every time anyway: name, date of birth, American? You're an American tourist?

They would say, "We don't even have room in our shelters for our own French people. We're here to help people who live in France. If we helped tourists, people would be using our shelters to vacation in." One operator even told me not to call 115 anymore. She said, "It's not for Americans."

I said, "Look, I'm not a tourist anymore. I'm really stuck here. I have no place to go and I'm walking all night because it isn't safe to stop. I can't keep walking, so I need a place to stay. Please help me."

But they kept saying, "No, you don't call this number. You're a tourist. This is for people who live in France." They told me that repeatedly.

One time I asked the guy, "If you have a file that comes up on your computer screen, why do I have to repeat it every day?" He said it was just the way they did it, and if the operators knew all the beds in the shelters were full and they heard a foreigner on the phone, they might not even pull up the file, because there wasn't even room for their own French people.

⚜ ⚜ ⚜

That night I had no place to stay again, so I walked, and I had nowhere to go, just around and around the Louvre and up and down Rivoli. Walking helps keep you safe and warm, so I walked where there were cars and people around.

There are air vents in the sidewalk on Rivoli where you can warm your feet a little, but if you linger there, wolves will come up to you. You have to stay alert all the time and mind your surroundings, so I was careful to stay in well-lit places and not stop for very long. Weekends are safer because there are a lot of regular people out on the street till three or four in the morning, and that kind of deters the wolves.

I guess I walked the next night too; it all starts to blur in my mind. I learned to pace myself, that's how I think of it. I couldn't sleep or rest my body for very long, but there were times I could rest my mind—zone out, keep walking, and focus on each step as I was taking it, one foot in front of the other.

I went back to the homeless restaurant Tico had taken me to. I finally managed to find it, after I got lost a couple of times. But the guy at the door said no, I had to have a special ticket to get food. I don't know what Tico said to get me in that one time, but now that I was by myself, the answer was "no way."

My feet and my legs were in pain, and so was my stomach. Hunger hurts; it feels like something inside your belly is trying to gnaw its way out. I get really severe hunger pains. When I miss even one meal, I start feeling painful cramps, and they get more and more intense. I can hear my stomach rumbling and it gets so loud I know other people can hear it, too. But after a while, maybe two or three days, you get little breaks in between the pain. You can feel it all the time, but it fades more into the background. It does take a while for that to happen, and it's worse if you're walking, because the spasms seem to go on for longer. And then even when the hunger does go away for a little while, it always comes back with a vengeance.

Sometimes I'd be walking hungry all night, then at some point I'd find some food and think, "OK, maybe it's time for me to eat now." I'd found a tangerine on the street; there were a surprising number of tangerines around. I guess they give them out a lot at homeless restaurants in December. In France they're like a Christmas thing.

One time I found two store-bought containers of ratatouille sitting on a bench at a bus stop. They were past their sell-by date, but somebody took the trouble to leave them there still sealed, nice and clean, for a hungry person to pick up. I was just so hungry that I ate one immediately, and I took the other one to Agora to eat with my café.

A woman that worked at Agora looked down her nose at me and said in this real scornful tone, "This is France. We don't eat stuff like that for breakfast." Like if I was in the United States, I'd be eating ratatouille for breakfast! I was broke and hungry and I found it on a bench at a bus stop, so I figured it was meant for me to eat, but I guess that was too much for her to understand.

Another time I found a whole slice of Brie, wrapped, sitting on a ledge beside the statues of the lions. Cheese is different in France. Some of it is real rich and good even though a lot of the cheeses smell so bad they make me nauseous. The Brie was amazing.

I never hunted through garbage. . . well, not exactly. But sometimes I'd see good food poking out of a pile of garbage, like outside a supermarket, and eat what was there, sticking out or on top. That's another lesson in humility.

But I never begged for money. I just didn't feel ready to do that. I felt like I could deal with a little hunger. It wasn't like I was going to starve to death overnight. Some people really do look like they're starving, and I was carrying some weight on me. That's what I used to tell myself: "I can miss a few meals and I'm not going to die." I used to fast when I was younger, just go without food for a day or two, so even though it was painful, I wasn't really frightened of hunger. I'd think about how Gandhi's mother fasted for no particular reason, and tell myself, "Hunger is enlightening, maybe I need to go for a while without food."

4

Walking

Gradually I fell into a routine. Tico had shown me some good resources. There were the free showers opposite the Centre Pompidou: Every morning they were open, I'd be there at eight. They only let you stay for fifteen minutes, and then they'd knock on the door and ask you to get out, but when you're really cold, a hot shower can really warm you up. Then I would go to Agora and try to get a table to lay my head on, and get coffee and bread if they had it.

The weather was really cold and wet. People said it was the worst winter Paris had seen in over twenty years, so it was difficult to stay dry and warm. I had a black coat that was kind of water repellent, but I lost my umbrella when I left it at the hostel. Of course, getting wet makes you colder, but I had to keep walking even when it rained. Sometimes I felt like I was soaked to the bone. It rains a lot in Oregon, and gets cold too, but I saw more snow and ice my first winter in Paris than I'd seen in the past ten years in Oregon. And in Oregon I always had an apartment or a room for rent, somewhere I could get warm and dry off and of course sleep.

I used to wash my clothes in the shower and take them back to Agora and hang them on a chair by the radiators to dry. It seemed like a lot of people did that at Agora, and they plugged their cell phones into the wall too; and nobody seemed to mind. Then I'd have coffee. It was great coffee at Agora, way better than normal coffee in America, as good as Starbucks. Even at Montesquieu the coffee was good. That was a nice surprise, that all the homeless places in Paris have such superior café.

You had to speak French, though—*café, sucre, merci,*—but I could manage the basic words. And at Agora the toilet was locked and you had to ask for the key to it in French, so I learned to say "*Je voudrais toilet clé, s'il vous plait.*" That's the French equivalent of "I would like the toilet key, please." That was probably my first French sentence. If you don't pronounce it correctly, or with too much of an accent other than French, sometimes they'll act like they don't understand you. Sometimes you have to ask three or four people before someone ends up giving you the key.

That's their thing: They'll only speak to you in French. They think if you only hear French, you're going to learn the language that way. But it doesn't work for me. It's all one big blur. I need to understand what the sentence means, or I learn nothing and don't know when to use that phrase again. For example, if I came up to you, a French or English speaker, and I only spoke to you in Chinese, would you learn Chinese? Their whole logic seems faulty to me.

And if they don't give you the key to the toilet, maybe they really don't know where it is, or maybe they really can't understand your French pronunciation, or maybe they're just messing with you, but there's always the magic toilet about two blocks away.

⚜ ⚜ ⚜

We were allowed to use the computer at Agora for half an hour or an hour, depending on who was in charge that day. So when I could get some time on it, I tried to access the balance on my prepaid credit card, hoping there was going to be enough on it to pay for a ticket out.

One day, the website worked. I was using the same password I always had, but it was the first time I tried from Agora. Maybe the Internet café had some kind of security lock that wouldn't let me access it.

There was only a little over $200 left. I just couldn't believe it. They had taken out the full fare of the first ticket, plus hundreds of dollars in taxes and fees, and there was a penalty fee for the second ticket because I had insufficient funds to cover it. All together they had taken nearly $800 U.S. dollars off my card. I remember thinking that was enough to pay for a ticket right there.

I just couldn't believe they could do that when I didn't even get a plane ticket. I was in shock again as I realized I was stuck here, really stuck. I had no idea how to get back home, or what I should do.

I tried the prepaid card at the next cash machine I saw, so at least I could have money for food, but it didn't work. The machine said something in French, and it wouldn't give me any money. I tried another bank and it did the same thing. It looked like my prepaid card didn't work in Europe, either.

⚜ ⚜ ⚜

Every day I'd call 115, and it was always the same runaround. I would ask them to please let me have a bed at Montesquieu and they would say they were full and I was an American tourist. I would try to explain it wasn't safe out there for a woman alone, but it was almost always no.

Every night I would go back to Montesquieu when the shelter opened at nine and ask them to let me in. I'd try to explain it wasn't safe for me on the street alone, and I'd even offer to sleep on the floor. Sometimes they would stop me and say, "No ticket, no bed," like it was some kind of mantra. Or they would say, "No English," and they almost always said, "*Parlez Francais*" (Speak French). Sure, I'm walking on the streets all night just to survive, and they expected me to learn one of the most difficult languages on the planet overnight with no teacher or resources.

About every two or three nights someone would relent and I'd get a place to sleep, or at least sit or lie down out of the weather. It was usually just one of the black vinyl armchairs, or sometimes one of the canvas cots, and they were pretty dirty. I don't think they ever washed the blankets at Montesquieu. People used to joke about something called the Montesquieu Itch. I did get a rash one time, but I don't think it was scabies, because it went away on its own eventually, so I was lucky there too.

On cold nights the cots were crammed together so tightly the men on either side of you could just stretch their arms out and reach for you. I would fall asleep and then startle awake, feeling as if someone had just grabbed me, and jump up in a panic, like it wasn't safe and I had to move. I was grabbing sleep like an animal, always half awake.

I think the longest I went without any sleep at all, just walking, was three days. I know I spent three days without eating much; that happened several times, and the nights were cold and long, so I was always glad if I got into Montesquieu. Even if I couldn't sleep much, at least it was a place out of the weather, where I could rest and get warm.

If they didn't let me in at nine, I would just circle for a while through the neighborhood. I always hoped someone would look out a window of the large Montesquieu building and see me walking. I hoped they would open a window or door and say, "It's OK, you've walked long enough, you can come inside now." But that never happened.

One night when I was safe inside Montesquieu, I heard a woman crying on the pavement after they turned her away. She was howling, banging on the door and shouting. That's a tough thing, to have to listen to somebody in that situation when you're safe inside. I felt her pain, and I knew what she was going to have to go through if they didn't let her in—survive the night, survive the wolves.

They did let her in eventually. One man told me that if you're a woman and you sit outside the door of Montesquieu or some other homeless shelter and cry and howl and beg, it may be midnight or one in the morning before they let you in, but they will do it. He said they would never make a woman stay out all night, because nobody wants to hear that you've been attacked or raped.

But I knew that wasn't true, because sometimes I would spend half the night outside Montesquieu and they didn't let me in.

I saw the woman again a few times. She was one of the few women I regularly saw at Montesquieu, but she was French, so I guess they let her in more often than me. She was usually a very quiet person, but I understood her fear and I knew why she had been so loud at the door. I felt a real connection with her after that night.

Her name was Marie and she always had a long cloth wrapped around her head, like a turban. I guess she was in her forties, but it's hard to tell with people who've been on the street. They can look a lot older than they are; it's a difficult way to survive. When you're in the same situation, you get to know each other even if you don't speak the same language. We never spoke, but we'd nod and smile at each other.

Maybe Marie even had a job. There were one or two other people at Montesquieu who seemed to take a lot of trouble with their appearance and left early, rushing off even before breakfast, like they had somewhere important they had to go.

I was just the opposite. Often the breakfast I had at Montesquieu was the only food I would get for a whole day or more. You got bread, butter, jam if they had it, and café—not what we'd call breakfast in America, but I got used to it. I ate a lot of bread and sugar—I'd butter the bread and put sugar cubes on it and drop a little coffee on top, and kind of melt it in with a spoon to make coffee syrup. It's good, and it keeps you going for a little while.

I noticed other people taking extra bread and butter and putting it in their bags. I was raised properly, and normally I'd never take something that wasn't offered to me, but I didn't know if I would get anything else to eat all day, and nobody seemed to mind, so I did it too.

⚜ ⚜ ⚜

At first I spent a lot of time near the Eiffel Tower. At night I would go and watch the light show that happens on the hour. I especially liked the lights that made the tower seem cobalt blue; it's such a soothing color. I liked how it shimmered and twinkled, and how from right underneath it there was a maze of lights over my head. And there's a merry-go-round down there; they light it up in the evening, and it goes round, empty most of the time, playing this tinny music in the dark. It's a lovely thing that brings you back to the present moment.

But the Eiffel Tower can get pretty spooky when they turn out all the lights. One night I was delirious from hunger and lack of sleep, and I remember walking away from the Eiffel Tower after they switched the lights out. The cobalt blue had turned a hard, dark gray, and it seemed like the tower had come alive in the dark, like a huge iron monster. I started walking away fast and I had to keep checking over my shoulder to make sure it wasn't following me.

After that I didn't head over to the Eiffel Tower as often, and this one man began to stalk me. It seemed like he was there most of the time, and he became hard to shake off. It frightened me, so I stopped going there at night.

I had some regular routes. I used to head from the statues of the lions to the Louvre and cross over the river on the wooden footbridge near the big clock. Then I'd walk over near the hostel I stayed at, by Pont Marie. That's a pretty bridge too, real sweet and simple. Or if it wasn't too late or too dark, I'd keep walking till I got to the gold angel at the place de la Bastille and try to take a rest over by the water, then turn around and walk back.

There's another bridge down from the Louvre where this big boat is docked, and they had parties on deck every weekend. It was too cold to stop for long, but I would linger for a while on the bridge, or by the waterfront, and watch the people dancing and laughing and having fun.

I spent a lot of time around the Louvre, in the courtyard and the gardens. In the daytime the Louvre is a good place to be. You can get a little shelter from the rain under the archway that leads to the courtyard, and watch the rain falling on the statues outside.

There was a huge Ferris wheel near the Tuileries Garden, close to the Louvre. Someone told me it was set up for the holidays, and they take it down after. It had individual compartments enclosed behind glass, like little cable cars—not like Ferris wheels in America, where the cars are open. One of the compartments even said "VIP," and it had tinted windows. I used to imagine riding that wheel one day. I'd think about how secure and also free it would feel in there, soaring over the rooftops.

I sighed, thinking about the holidays, and I remembered one of my favorite Christmas mornings. I was about eight years old, and

I had always loved animals, especially horses. I had a model horse collection. While most little girls my age played with their Barbie dolls, I played with my horses. After Thanksgiving, my mom took me to the toy store and said, "We aren't buying anything, just getting ideas for Christmas."

They had gotten some new model horses in behind the glass counter, and there was one that stood out. It was a dark bay with a black mane and tail made of hair you could comb. The lady behind the counter handed it to me. It wore a real leather bridle and saddle, and you could hear the leather squeak when you adjusted them.

I dreamed about that horse until Christmas morning, when I rushed to the Christmas tree, picking up all the packages with my name on them, till I found one about the size of the horse. I ripped it open, and there it was! The horse I had been dreaming of. I played with it for hours each day. I'd comb its mane and tail and practice adjusting the saddle and bridle, so that when I got a real horse, I'd know how. I would fall asleep with it in my arms and dream it was real.

❖ ❖ ❖

But you have to stay alert, even around the Ferris wheel and the Louvre. There are lots of guards, and beggars too. Of course, they can spot a foreigner in a second. At first the gypsy women with long skirts would try the gold-ring trick on me. They'll pretend to pick up a gold ring (it's actually a plastic ring covered with gold paper), and hand it to you like they think you've dropped it, and then they ask you for money. I got that one a lot, and when I explained, "No euro," they'd get mad and yell at me because I was wise to the game.

But after a few weeks, they stopped yelling. They'd still try the gold-ring trick, and I'd still say "no euro," but we would smile at each other like we both understood—nobody's at fault here, we're all the same, just trying to survive.

❖ ❖ ❖

The second week I was in Paris, I spent maybe three nights in Montesquieu. Then for a while I didn't get in at all—maybe the place was full because it was so cold. On those nights, I mostly walked up and down rue de Rivoli. It's fairly safe most of the time because it's well lit, and if you walk under the archways, where all the tourist shops are, you can stay dry. Even in November there are tourists, and on weekends there'll be a few regular people walking around Rivoli until four or five in the morning. That keeps you a little bit safer.

I got used to seeing the regular homeless people sleeping every night in the same places along Rivoli, like it was their patch of ground. Almost all of them were men. Homeless women have to find a really good hiding place if they're going to get any sleep, or the wolves will get them.

I remember the first time I realized that in one of the sleeping bags, hunched beside the buildings down around the Hotel Meurice, there was a woman. She had light brown hair and looked like she was a bit younger than me. I was shocked. I looped past a couple of times, just to check up on her, but there were two men sleeping in bags, one on either side of her, so I guess she was OK.

I couldn't risk sleeping out in the open, and it was way too cold to sleep without a sleeping bag, so I just had to keep walking.

Sometimes I would walk through the little neighborhoods around the statue on Place des Victoires, north of the big mall at Les Halles, and I would wish for my own little window. The kind that open up like little French doors, and those thin curtains where you can't really see in, you can only make out the shadows. A little apartment, with a little French window and balcony, a safe place of my own where I could get out of the weather and prop my feet up, where the wolves couldn't touch me.

5

Resisting

At first I didn't spend long periods of time at Agora, because it didn't feel very safe there. Even though the nonprofit organization that ran the place, Emmaus, had workers and volunteers there to watch over things, it was a pretty rough bunch of people who hung out there. I got stared at and questioned a lot by the other homeless people, but never by the social workers. I guess they figured they were being respectful, that we were tired and had a lot to deal with. None of them asked me any questions, and when I went up and tried to talk with them, they always said nobody spoke English. Their attitude was basically that I was a nuisance, and if they ignored me, I would eventually go away.

There weren't many women at Agora. There were maybe a few more than at the shelter on rue Montesquieu, but not a lot, and no children. There's no way they'd let children in there.

I'd say well over half of the men looked like they weren't French or from Western Europe. Mostly they were from Arab and African countries, but there were some Chinese people and a lot of people from Eastern Europe too, and they always spoke a little English.

The first thing I learned was to identify the ones that seemed mentally unstable—the ones that looked like they might be drunk, or like they were permanently on the edge of exploding into violence.

There appeared to be a lot of unstable people at Agora and I guess maybe some of them had checkered pasts.

I remember one young guy, kind of punky, just started screaming one afternoon. He had a shaved head with only a topknot of hair, and he smelled pretty ripe. They had to wrestle him out.

Guys would fight all the time or they'd get drunk, except some strict Muslim men, and they'd start yelling and hitting the walls. Some of them would do it every few days and the social worker would escort them out, but the next day they would almost always be back.

Sometimes the police would come. One time an older guy with short gray hair, who seemed to be French, got mad at the people who worked at Agora. One night he hit a couple of them and started smashing stuff and overturning tables, so they called the police.

Before they arrived, a lot of men just melted away. I left too. I was afraid to stick around and see what would happen next. I could just picture that scene in America; if the police tried to arrest the guy and he resisted, they would have tasered him to the ground, or worse. There's a lot of aggressive behavior and power and control in the police force in America. I've seen it. In Portland, the police shot and killed a homeless man. They said he was behaving aggressively, but witnesses said he wasn't.

So I was very surprised to see that same guy in Les Halles park later that night. It made me realize the police in France aren't as aggressive as they are in America. They don't appear to abuse their power the same way.

⚜ ⚜ ⚜

At Agora there was one group of Arab men who kept to themselves. They never spoke to me, but their eyes said they wanted nothing to do with me. Maybe it was because I was American, or because I was an American woman, or maybe just any kind of Western woman. I'm not sure.

But quite a lot of the homeless people spoke English. Many people in France can speak a little English if they want to, especially the foreigners. After a while I started to feel like a lot of the homeless men at Agora weren't a threat. They'd often come up and talk to me, and sometimes they didn't make much sense, but they didn't necessarily mean any harm.

Or I could manage them. There was one Asian guy, and he'd always be friendly and smile, but then he'd try and push against me or touch my breasts, but I'd say no very firmly and he'd kind of laugh and back off.

So there were wolves at Agora, but they were like respectful, domesticated wolves. They made it difficult for me to lay my head down and rest. But eventually, if I was polite but firm to them, and clear enough about saying no, they'd move away.

One guy was even kind of funny—a young Algerian man, maybe twenty-five years old, named Salim. He had his friend François, who spoke some English, come over and translate that he loved me and wanted to marry me. It was pretty amusing. I said, "Tell him he's too young for me," and Francois said, "What about me? I'm older." I smiled and we joked around for a little bit.

After that, whenever Salim saw me at Agora, he would make a heart sign with his hands in front of his chest and kind of throb it at me and greet me: "My GIRLFRIEND!" It was cute; it wasn't threatening.

One time, Salim got me a chair to sit on from the office—I wouldn't have dared to do that. Then he sat me down beside him and he pulled out a porn magazine. That was the most offensive thing he did and it wasn't that bad. I just said no and left.

⚜ ⚜ ⚜

I finally found out how to get the money out of my prepaid credit card. I was trying it again at a cash machine, and a woman nearby realized I was a foreigner. She spoke good English. She said the same thing had happened to her too, and that I had to find a bank that was run by the government if I wanted to make a foreign credit card work. She pointed to a bank down the road—we were on Avenue de l'Opéra. Finally I could withdraw money from the card. The bank wouldn't let me take all of it out, but I took as much as I could. After converting the dollars to euros and then calculating bank commissions, it came to 180 euros. I realized later that I had to have at least twenty euros left on the card to withdraw money, and that's why it wouldn't let me take it all out.

It went fast. I decided to buy two nights at the hostel, but I spread them out—walk a couple of nights, get a room. I bought some metro tickets too, so I could ride around on the subway to get out of the weather and dry off. Sometimes I catnapped on the metro too. I think I ate a couple of times at McDonalds: It's only ninety-five cents for a hamburger and ninety-nine cents for fries. I also bought some cans of sardines. You can have a whole can for fifty-four cents, in tomato sauce or with olive oil, and with a little bread that's a high-protein meal that will keep you going when you're hungry.

I remember a charge nurse I worked with at Providence St. Vincent Medical Center in Oregon who used to eat sardines every day for lunch. One day someone commented, "You really like sardines," and she explained, "They're cheap, they're a good source of protein and omega-3, and if you eat the bones, calcium, and if you take the scales off, they aren't that bad."

But her main reason was they're very cheap, and she was right about that. Before I came to France, I couldn't eat them, but now I even eat the bones. And just in case I get in a bind for food, I always like to know there's a can or two on the shelf.

I could also see the phone card I'd bought a few weeks back was never going to work. I had shown someone at Agora my Google phone and he told me I should buy a European SIM card and then it should work. So, once I had some money, I bought an Orange SIM card for twenty-five euros and put it in the phone, but it still didn't work.

It was an American phone, so it was locked and would only work with American T-Mobile, and it didn't look like they were ever going to email me back.

I also bought a pack of cigarettes. There's cigarette smoke all over Paris, and when I first arrived in town, it drove me nuts. They say more than a third of adults smoke in France, and I'm not sure what the proportion is in Oregon, but it's certainly lower. I used to smoke a little when I was younger, and I realized that although cigarette smoke really bothered me, if I smoked, it didn't—and people at Agora were always offering me cigarettes. When you get really hungry, and have no money or meal ticket, and you're new on the street and can't find food, cigarettes help with the hunger pains. So I guess I picked up the taste for it again.

Several times men offered to buy me a meal, but I was afraid they would get the wrong idea, that they would expect me to have sex with them if I let them buy me food. As hungry as I was, I would never do that.

You have to understand how different the culture is in Europe. In America, a woman can meet a man and have dinner with him, and if he makes advances and she says no, that's it. No means no. But in Europe, it's different; it's almost like going back in time to the 1950s in America. People don't listen to women like they do to men, and I can definitely see how date rape happens over here, because almost everyone takes the man's word over the woman's— as you will see later on.

I also learned the wolves will put stuff in your drink. I used to carry a bottle of water and fill it up at the fountain in Agora, and one time I left it on the table while I went to get café. When I came back, this Croatian guy told me to never do that, that men would slip drugs into a woman's drink, they did it all the time.

I was offered alcohol too. It seemed like someone was always drinking outside Agora. I guess you can pretty much drink openly on the street in France. Once you get to be a familiar face, they'll just nudge the bottle at you, like, go ahead.

But I never felt like drinking. I knew I needed to be sharp and alert all the time, and able to walk all night. If you've drunk some wine and you're tired, you can't do that. It would be like asking to be attacked.

⚜ ⚜ ⚜

It snowed the weekend before Thanksgiving, and one of the guys who worked at Montesquieu let me have a cot there for two nights running. Actually, I think they let everyone in when it snows, but this guy, Mohamed, seemed like a really good person, so I started keeping an eye out for him. He was the only one who consistently acted like I was just a human being in need. For the others, it was just random, and mostly "No American tourist," but if Mohamed was at the door, he'd usually let me in.

On one of the nights it snowed, there was an elderly gentleman lying near me with what looked like a pretty serious case of congestive heart failure. I've seen it in nursing homes, and once you get to a certain stage, you can't lie down and sleep anymore. You have to sit up because your body is pretty much drowning in its own fluids.

He had propped himself up on the couch, and his legs were very swollen, with sores that had swelled up so much they had busted open, and they had a really strong odor. A lot of people at Montesquieu smelled bad, whether from alcohol or just body odors, but this guy was really ill.

Somebody talked to him. It sounded like they were trying to get him to go to the hospital, but he didn't want to go. He sat up on a couch breathing very heavily and looked like he'd given up, and he coughed stuff up all night as he struggled to breathe. I felt his pain and wanted to help him, but I sensed it was beyond me.

I wanted to sleep on that couch one night, but Mohamed told me, "Not that one, you don't want to sleep there." From the way he was talking, I guessed there were bugs on it. It was pretty ragged, but it looked a lot more comfortable than the cots.

⚜ ⚜ ⚜

A guy at Agora said that maybe I could pay an extra fee to unlock my Google phone online, so I found a website that said it would cost twelve euros, and I knew there was that much left on the card, but less than twenty euros, since I couldn't access the money. I clicked yes and they sent a confirmation, but the code never came. I emailed them repeatedly, but they never sent it, and that was how I spent the last of my money.

⚜ ⚜ ⚜

The cold weather, the wolves, and the pain: every night was a fight for survival. There were moments of despair, when I felt like I couldn't take much more. One night I was in so much pain I remember thinking that if I could just figure out how to get up the

Eiffel Tower, I could jump off. I was freezing and hurting so bad, and I couldn't rest, or even think about sleeping, because when I sat down the wolves wouldn't leave me alone.

But I guess I knew if I could just make it till the next morning, I could go to Agora, and there'd be other people in similar circumstances. Maybe most of the men at Agora could get by, because they could find spaces to sleep in underground parking lots or in the metro tunnels. But the few women that were at Agora, well . . . life was rough for all of us.

6

Awareness of Reacting

You have probably been thinking that I should have gone to the U.S. Embassy, and maybe they would have helped me out. But I didn't know how embassies worked back then—I had never left America before, so I didn't need to know that.

Every so often I would come across someone who spoke enough English to strike up a conversation. One night I was waiting in line to try and get into Montesquieu when this man started talking to me. He said he was French, but he lived in Jamaica with his mother. He came back to France to do some kind of business deal, and 115 had given him the runaround at first too, saying all the shelters were full. And he was French—he even showed me his ID card.

A lot of the men did that, like you were supposed to be impressed they were French. Some of them told me they used to work and got a small check every month from the government, so they could at least buy some food. Maybe they thought it proved they could be a good provider, and some of them asked if they could be my boyfriend.

I was just trying to survive. The last thing I wanted was a boyfriend. I couldn't see beyond surviving the next day.

I was really pretty sick by this time. After days and nights of walking, my cold had gotten much worse. The Jamaican guy said, "You got the grip, huh?" I was like, "*What?*" I thought he meant some sexually transmitted disease or something, so I said, "No way!"

He laughed and said, "You really don't speak one word of French, do you?" Because *grippe*—they pronounce it "grip"—means the flu in French, but to me it sounded like something out of a Stephen King novel: the grip of death. There was even a Stephen King novel and movie, *The Stand*, where a strain of super-flu called Captain Trips wipes out most of the population. Then he asked if I had paracetamol—that's the French equivalent of Tylenol—and gave me some. It was sealed in individual packages, so I figured it would be safe.

I didn't get into Montesquieu that night, and the Jamaican guy did, but he was French. He showed me a voucher he got from a social worker, so he could stay at Montesquieu for two or three weeks. Before he went in, he told me that he needed someone who spoke English to help translate with his business deal. It was some kind of website, but I had trouble understanding him. At first I thought maybe it was a legitimate transaction, and I needed to make money for a plane ticket home, so I hoped this would be a good start.

I met him the next day in front of the Centre Pompidou to try to work it out, but when he started explaining the deal to me, he kept getting confused. I realized after a little while that although he seemed very sincere, and always was kind and respectful to me, he wasn't completely mentally stable, and his deal was pretty much a scam. He showed me a letter he had, and it was on a letterhead with a French flag. Of course I couldn't understand what it said, but he said it was signed by some big French politician. Then he admitted to me that he'd typed the letter up on his computer at home, to help him get the money together for his deal.

Jamaica was a resourceful guy. I stopped seeing him around after a little while, so who knows, maybe he did get something off the ground.

On Thanksgiving Day, I walked past a couple of restaurants in Les Halles that were advertising special American turkey dinners, but that's all there was. Other than that, in France, Thanksgiving was just a normal working day. I knew that, but when you live all your life celebrating this one day every year, it's strange to suddenly not acknowledge it.

If I was back home in Portland, I probably would have worked. I got paid time and a half for working holidays. Still, depending on which shift, I would have watched the Macy's Thanksgiving Day Parade on TV in the morning, or football in the afternoon, and Chloe and I would have organized it so we could eat turkey together at some point.

I pictured Chloe and Carlos and his brother sitting around the table to eat a spicy turkey dinner. I went all the way and imagined a really beautifully decorated table with lit candles on it. The meal would have included spicy turkey, stuffing, mashed potatoes, cranberry sauce, and sweet-potato pie for dessert—many of the things my mom used to make.

It was all so far away.

There had to be a way out of this.

⚜ ⚜ ⚜

I emailed the nursing agency I worked for back in Portland, and I asked them to check my last paycheck, because I thought I was missing some money. This was pretty much my last hope, but they said I'd have to contact payroll because they didn't have time to deal with it, and things were crazy in the office as usual. I tried to explain I was getting desperate, but it seemed like they never understood the severity of the situation.

I couldn't think what else to do. Chloe didn't have email and I couldn't phone her. So I asked the agency to call and ask Chloe to send me some money. I said that maybe she could send some of the rent money I'd given her for December, because I needed it real bad.

The nursing agency answered back that Chloe was wiring me some money through Western Union, but that took days. I remember I went to the Western Union office on rue Saint-Denis and they said Chloe had sent me some money but I couldn't get it until I told them the code. They had asked her a question and there was a code word I needed to give them.

So I emailed the nursing agency and asked if they could please call Chloe and ask her for the code, and we went back and forth for a few days.

Finally the nursing agency emailed me and said that nobody had asked Chloe a question, there was no code. I went back and told Western Union there was no code, and the guy smiled like it was some kind of joke, and gave me $100. I stretched it out as long as I could.

⚜ ⚜ ⚜

There was an old African man who used to sit on an air vent outside the McDonald's on Rivoli, not far from Agora. He had gray hair and a little beard, and he was in pretty rough shape. He would always leave a paper cup out for people to put money in, and I noticed that even when he fell asleep, nobody would ever steal it. I liked that. In America somebody would have taken the money for sure.

It got so we would nod and smile at each other, and maybe stop and say hi. He was Nigerian, so he spoke English, but it was just a little difficult to follow him sometimes.

One time it had been raining and it was cold like usual, and he said, "Come on, sit down, it's warmer here." So I sat on the vent with him for maybe an hour or two and warmed my feet. He showed me a book where he'd drawn some pictures, and photographs of his mother in Nigeria. He shared his food with me. It was half an egg sandwich with mayonnaise. I'm a nursing assistant, so I was thinking, how long had that sandwich been around? I bit into it anyway because I was really hungry, but it was so warm, and it had a lot of mayo on it—I just couldn't do it. But I didn't want to offend him, so I stashed it and fed it to the pigeons later on.

It was remarkable to see the reactions of the people passing by. When you're sitting on an air vent with an old African guy in dirty clothes, people judge you. They look down at you; they sneer and stare at you like you're insulting them by just sitting there and talking.

After that he always spoke to me when I came by, and wanted me to sit down, but he didn't seem too stable, so I thought it might be better to keep a little space between us. But I would always stop for a while to say hi and see how he was doing.

Once Tico saw me in the street talking to him, and he hustled me off and said, "Do you know what that looks like? You shouldn't be talking to those people." Tico was homeless too, but I guess he saw himself as better or different than other homeless people. It wasn't about race, because Tico was black too, but he said, "Those people are different."

I said, "They're not that different, you know? You go sit there for an hour, and talk, and look at his books and photos of his mother in Africa, and see what you feel like."

Tico asked if I had filed the form I was given, the first day we were looking for domiciles, and I said no, because I didn't really understand it. There was a note of explanation about the form in French that was three pages long and just a couple of paragraphs in English. It said if you signed this form and turned it in, the French government could give you three hundred euros a month or some kind of housing, but if you refused the housing they wouldn't give you the money.

The English part didn't say you were filing to be a political refugee from your government. The man who gave it to me said I should fill it out and hand it in at a police station, way up northeast of town near Porte de la Villette. There's a really big park close by that has this huge silver ball with a museum inside. If you have some money to spend, you can go inside the ball and walk around. Tico had shown me the metro stop on my map, and he wanted to come with me, but I told him, no, I'd find it myself. I went alone the next morning, but I got lost, and by the time I got there it was too late to turn in the paperwork, so they told me to come back at seven thirty the next morning.

So I went back in the morning, and took a number and waited. I was called up to a window where I had to show my passport to the lady behind the glass. She stamped the paperwork and said something in French. I didn't understand, so she motioned like being fingerprinted, and pointed to the other side of the room. I went over there and waited till they called my name. They fingerprinted me and gave me an appointment to come back.

I still didn't really know what all this was about and it bothered me that I didn't understand what the forms really meant or what I was signing. So I kept the paperwork on me for a few days, hoping somebody at Agora would be able to translate it for me properly. There was one guy who used to show up there from time to time— he was a homeless person, but he always had a briefcase, and he used to help the other homeless people with their paperwork, for doctors' appointments and social workers and so on.

He spoke Arabic, French, English, and Urdu, and I used to call him the paperwork guy. He said he was from Pakistan and he had curly hair that sometimes he would lighten a bit. He was very creative, and I always liked him. You could tell he was well educated. I saw him a couple of times giving free advice to men trying to win over a woman. He just liked to help people and never asked for anything in return.

The paperwork guy wasn't around at Agora, but a couple of days later Tico showed up there again and said now he'd made an appointment for me to find a job. I thought it would be some kind of interview, so I tried to look nice.

But actually the woman was some kind of specialized social worker. She was a nice-looking woman in her forties with short, curly hair, and it seemed like she wasn't barking at me like most of the people who worked at Agora did. Her work seemed to be to figure out what I could do to get a job. She suggested I could print out some fliers to teach English and stick them up at schools, or maybe find work as a nanny.

Before that, none of the social workers I'd approached would speak to me. When I was at Agora, they seemed annoyed by the simple fact that I couldn't speak French in order to explain my situation to them. I was well respected by my fellow workers and friends in the United States, so to be disrespected to this point was a bad experience for me.

If I managed to get someone to talk to me, they'd all claim to speak no English. But I found out afterward they didn't all feel obliged to tell the truth about that. Months later, I was still trying to get a domicile, so I asked one of the newer social workers—his head was shaved and he admitted he spoke a little English. He said, "Oh, it's my colleague there who looks after that."

"Well, does he speak any English?" I asked, and the bald guy called out his colleague's name and said, in English, "Do you speak English for this person today?" Then they both laughed.

It was a very sad and frustrating situation. These people weren't there to sincerely help us; they were just playing games with us. I was freezing, had no money left, and really needed assistance, and maybe because I was American, they treated me like I was some kind of joke.

❖ ❖ ❖

The curly-haired woman at the job office really took the time to explain things. I gave her the form I had kept with me to look at, and she was horrified. She told me I wasn't a refugee and this was truly a bad idea. It was like saying you were a traitor to America. If I signed it, with the Patriot Act, the U.S. government could even put me on a terrorist watch list.

I was shocked. I had no idea. The few people that had looked at it had just kept referring me to the few paragraphs in English, and it said nothing like that—just that they would help me find a place to stay or give me three hundred euros a month. So the woman called the phone number on the form and asked them what to do. They told her to write "ERROR" across it, so she did, and I never went back for the interview.

She also explained what a domicile was, which I'd pretty much already figured out by this point. Then she called around and made me an appointment to get a domicile, but when I went there, it was the same story: We're full, check back in two weeks.

But above all, that woman was the first person who suggested that I should go to the U.S. Embassy. I guess that was at the beginning of December, sometime after Thanksgiving, and maybe she just took pity on me, because I'd been on the street, in the cold, for about three weeks. Probably no more than five nights of that was spent in Montesquieu, which wasn't exactly restful either. I was truly exhausted and I suppose she could tell.

She wrote down "U.S. Embassy" and the street address on a piece of paper, and I went over there right away. It was on a little street just off Rivoli, up near where the Ferris wheel was set up. I had walked almost right past it probably close to a hundred times, and didn't even know.

I got through security, which was a big deal—there were guards, and they took everything out of my purse and pockets, bagged all of it in plastic, and stapled it shut with my name and ticket number on the label. Then I went up the stairs, took another ticket, and waited in a big room with lots of glass cubicles for my number to come up.

When my number came up, I went to the window and tried to explain the situation I was in, and that I needed help. I guess the woman had some kind of accent—she seemed to have trouble understanding what I was saying, and she was real short-tempered. I remember telling her, "I'm stuck here," that I was sleeping on the street, and that I needed to get back home. Maybe I said something about needing help to find a job, so I could make the money for the plane ticket.

This woman said, "You need to go to the French embassy." She said it three or four times. I pulled out my passport to show her I was an American citizen, but she said, "You're at the wrong place." Then she stood up and pointed me out the door. She was all but yelling at me.

I think this was the first time I really cried in France. The kind social worker had told me the U.S. Embassy should be able to help me. I went and washed my face and tried to calm down. I told myself, "It's OK, you just have to go across town or wherever the French embassy is."

See, everyone had been telling me, "You're in France now, this isn't America, you have to speak French. You're in France now, this isn't America, we only drink café after meals and we never drink milk after breakfast. You're in France now, you can't eat ratatouille for breakfast, even if you're starving." So, "You're in France now, you have to go to the French embassy." I know this may sound naive, but by this point, I had been told so many times, "No, this is France, you do it *this* way now," that I believed her. She was so angry, and she kept pointing at the door, nearly yelling that I had to leave, so I walked away. I didn't know what else to do.

At the doorway, as I was getting my belongings back from the guard on duty, I asked him, "Do you know where the closest French embassy is?"

He chuckled and said, "London."

I said "No, really, no joke, where's the nearest French embassy?"

He laughed loud at that and said, "Think about it. Is there an American embassy in America?"

I said I didn't know. I'd never tried to find an American embassy in America.

So he answered, "There's no French embassy in France. England's probably the closest place you'll find one."

I was astonished, and I didn't have money to go to the French embassy in England.

I was in a daze from exhaustion and lack of food, and I don't even remember walking back to Agora, but that's where I went. It seemed like the only warm place where I could sit down and rest.

I had no money in my pockets, nowhere to stay, and absolutely no idea what to do.

7

The Illusion of Control

I kept reading *A New Earth* by Eckhart Tolle. I always had it with me. Sometimes I would just read a few sentences, paragraphs, or pages. One day I ran across this quote:

"Life will give you whatever experience is most helpful for the evolution of your consciousness."

I marked that page and kept walking. Eckhart Tolle sat on a park bench for two years, and he used it for growth, so perhaps I could use my situation for growth too.

⚜ ⚜ ⚜

I was very hungry, and I had no money or meal ticket, so maybe a cigarette would temporarily help. Occasionally I would try to bum a cigarette from a stranger, but there's an easier solution. There are many smokers in France, and they have laws that you can't smoke in cafés and shops, so as a result people often throw away perfectly good cigs only half-smoked. If one breaks, they'll just throw it on the ground, and if it drops, sometimes they'll just leave it there.

Their trash was my treasure. Looking for cigarettes gave me something to focus on. You have a few options when you find a half-smoked cig on the ground. You can pick it up and smoke it right off, but you might catch something—the cotton filter can hold on to bacteria and viruses for a while.

But most bacteria and viruses can't survive in sunlight and air for very long, so the paper around the filter is usually pretty safe. So you take the cig, wipe off the outside paper, pull out the cotton filter, and smoke it that way.

Or you can break the filter completely off, empty the tobacco into a bag, and reroll your tobacco. I did it the French way, rolling up a little piece of cardboard as a filter so it would hold right. You bum the cigarette paper from someone, or if you have a little money, buy some—it only costs one euro and twenty cents for one hundred papers, so even if you're a true addict, you're not spending much more than a euro a week.

This last choice has other possibilities as well. I would break off the black end that had been burnt so it looked clean, and package the tobacco nicely in a little bag like you get when they sell loose tobacco. Sometimes I found them on the street, or someone at Agora would give me an empty one, and you can trade that, or sell it. Occasionally I'd sell a pouch for two or three euros per thirty-five to forty grams—when the bag is filled between one third and one half full. It didn't happen often because almost everyone knew where I got my tobacco, but sometimes they would trade with me, and turn right around and sell it to someone who didn't realize that the tobacco came directly from the streets of Paris.

I learned the hot spots for picking up cigs: metro entrances, waiting for the tram, outside tobacco shops, ATM machines, taxi stops, bus stops, and anywhere on the Champs-Élysées and other specific tourist shops. The neighborhoods were crucial as well. You can really tell the type of neighborhood by the cigs on the ground.

Around Republic, for example, there are a lot of bars and restaurants and buses, but there always are a lot of homeless people too, so there's seldom a usable cigarette on the ground. Poor people smoke every cigarette down to the butt. Champs-Élysées is the opposite: It's one of the hot spots, with lots of tourists walking in and out of shops and people who think nothing of throwing away half a cigarette. There are usually cigarillos and cigars too.

It was always nice to find a cigar: You can roll a lot of cigs from half a cigar. I would cut them up and stash the tobacco. When it rains, you can't pick up cigs because they are all wet, so when I ran out of tobacco, I would pull from my cigar stash, and roll the cigar tobacco into a cigarette.

Sometimes I'd go further afield. The 17th arrondissement is great, though it's a long walk to get there if you don't have a metro ticket. Almost every time I went there I'd easily pick up a day's supply of tobacco in half an hour. It appears to be a nicer neighborhood, and the kind of place people will nonchalantly throw a perfectly good cigarette on the ground.

In the beginning, I was careful how I'd pick the cigarette up. I'd use a distraction, like a bag or a tissue, and I'd set it down next to the cig and then scoop the cigarette up like I was doing nothing special. But then I started using it as a lesson in humility: I'd just bend over and pick it up, openly knowing that people would see me, and they were aware of what I was doing. I usually did it this way at least once a week, more often if I felt I needed it.

Try it, and you'll see people watching you and shaking their heads. They look at you with disgust. They're judging you, and you know that in your former life you probably would have thought it was disgusting too, but it's a good lesson in humility, very grounding. "For whoever exalts himself will be humbled, and whoever humbles himself will be exalted."

Every once in a while someone will sincerely surprise you. One night I was walking near the Gare d'Austerlitz, another railway station near the river. At a little restaurant-bar, I found three half-cigarettes close together. I was focused on the task at hand. I knew there were people in the bar, but I paid them no attention. I just picked up the three cigs and kept going. A few steps later this firm voice was yelling in French, "Hey! Wait a moment."

At first I thought he was mad at me for picking up the cigs, but I turned around and he had his pack of Camels open. He gave me a clean, fresh one. His unexpected generosity really moved me. I guess he caught me off guard, but I could feel his sincerity. The tears were leaking out by the time I reached the corner. I had to stop for a while and put some space between the emotions I was feeling and the moment.

Another time, one of the Polish guys from Agora saw me picking up a cigarette and I said, "You probably think this is disgusting."

He said no, he did it all the time. One night while lying down in the underground garage he used to sleep in, he saw someone throw a lit cigarette down from an upper floor. He made a beeline for it and another voice called out, "That one's mine!"

Picking up the cigarettes gave me something positive to focus on, plus it was a much-needed break from the weather, the pain, and the wolves. I was keeping my mind busy, focused on something productive, and after two or three days of hard work, I could pick up a bag of tobacco; that was something I could achieve. But most of all, it gave me the illusion of being in control of something.

⚜ ⚜ ⚜

One day I met a homeless man from Scotland in Agora. Thomas was a skinny little guy in jeans and boots, in his forties I'd guess, with sandy-colored hair. He didn't seem threatening; he seemed harmless and kind, and it was good just to talk to someone who spoke fluent English.

Thomas told me he'd come to France looking for work, because he had a European passport and he could work wherever he wanted. He never found a job, though he tried really hard to get one. They almost gave him a job handing out free newspapers by the metro entrance, but they said his French wasn't good enough even for that job, though it was a lot better than mine.

But Thomas said even if he didn't find a job, if he stayed for three months the French government would give him a check, four hundred euros a month, and if he was spending it all on rent, they'd give him another two hundred euros to live on. He said maybe it was only for European citizens, but he'd almost made it through his ninety days, and he just hoped it was true. He had a meal ticket—he could speak some French—but even I worried about him. He just had a thin fake-leather jacket and it was freezing at night, and he really did look like he was starving.

Sometimes he would sleep in one of the big underground parking lots on Sébastopol. Men can go and sleep down in garages and subway tunnels and be safe and warm, but not women: they'd be attacked in the blink of an eye. Then Thomas got a ticket to sleep for a month at a homeless shelter near Montparnasse, a shelter just for men. He said it wasn't great, but he was happy to be out of the cold.

Thomas showed up one day with a brand-new coat on. He said there was a place in Les Halles, on Rambuteau, where they would give you clothes. He showed me another place too, a big area near the Gare de l'Est railway station where a van would come by every night at seven thirty and people would give you food: coffee, and maybe soup or sometimes just food in cans.

That evening a young guy came staggering into Agora from outside. You could see he was really wobbly, and he grabbed onto the trashcan like he was going to vomit, and then just slumped down the wall and kind of sat there nodding. He was a skinny white guy in his twenties wearing a hoodie, and I assumed heroin by way he looked. Then all of a sudden he conked over like a stone onto the floor.

Thomas and I stared at him for a moment, and I said, "Is he breathing?"

Thomas said, "Hey, I don't know. That's your job."

So I went over to take a look. The guy did have a faint pulse and he was breathing, but shallowly, so I started patting his sternum, to try to wake him up. It took a while, but eventually he gasped and took a deep breath and woke up, surprised because there were several of us all around him. He seemed dazed, but he said he was OK, so I figured I would just let him be.

Some of the guys who worked at Agora saw him. They were standing around, and when he woke up they just said, "Tss," and walked off. I guess they see it a lot.

⚜ ⚜ ⚜

It was almost Christmas, and Paris was getting all dressed up with lights. There was a new ad for men's cologne on billboards all over town, and the model—although about twenty years younger— bore a striking resemblance to Alex back home in Portland. I'd be walking in the middle of the night, feeling as though I couldn't take another step, and I'd look up and see his face and hear his words: "Stop resisting, Ann."

Before I left, I asked him, "In your opinion, if I could only take one thing with me to Europe, what should I bring?"

He said, "Why take something with you that can be taken away? It's not what you carry with you, it's the way you handle situations that come up."

Then Alex gave me an analogy. He was backpacking in Europe, walking when he couldn't hitch a ride. He said at first his backpack was light and he didn't have any trouble walking. Then he started getting a lot of stuff and putting it in his backpack. It got so heavy and was weighing him down so much, he could barely walk.

Sometimes I would be so exhausted and in so much pain that I didn't think I could keep walking, and I'd catch sight of him. It was like those billboards would reorient me. They were like the Eiffel Tower: I'd catch sight of them at unexpected moments, at the corner of a street, and it was kind of like a silent message, to be present in this moment. "Everything happens that is supposed to happen. If you're there, that's where you're meant to be. Stop resisting. Surrender to the moment."

There were also posters up all over town advertising Euro Disney, and they had some special deal on for Christmas vacation. Sometimes at night, while I was walking past them, I'd hum the Mickey Mouse song. I love Disney. I'd imagine that Euro Disney would have a homeless day, when it would open its doors for free for homeless people, and I'd picture the people I'd met at Agora and on the street riding the rides there and having a ball.

I used to joke with Thomas that the one thing I really missed of all the possessions I left behind in Oregon were my Mickey Mouse ears. One day at the Eiffel Tower I was waiting in line for the toilet—there aren't many public toilets that I know of in that neighborhood—and this woman in front of me had the coolest furry hat. It went all the way down to her neck, it looked really warm, and it had Mickey Mouse ears, and I remember thinking, *That's exactly what I've been dreaming of.* While walking on the street and humming, I'd think about how I was going to make holes in a black stocking hat and stick Mickey Mouse ears through the holes, so I'd have warm Mickey Mouse ears too.

I liked that the Mouse was offering a joke about E-Mouse, Emmaus. That was the name of the organization that ran Agora and Montesquieu, so the Mouse always made me smile.

A lot of the stuff I'd brought with me was still in my suitcase back at the hostel. I went back there to get it after someone told me I could store it at Montesquieu, in the back room. They had my suitcase out in the lobby like they were getting ready to throw it out, so that was a lucky break.

I later found out the back room where they put my suitcase was unlocked to all the homeless women whenever Montesquieu was open for the women's group. Someone went through it and stole some stuff. They took my only other pair of pants, socks, and some makeup. At first I thought it was odd they didn't take the one dress I brought with me, but then I realized a dress wouldn't do a homeless woman much good in freezing weather. And not only would it make it easier for the wolves to attack her, it also had some shiny sequin flowers that would probably attract them.

❖ ❖ ❖

One morning towards the middle of December, they threw us out of Montesquieu as usual around a quarter after seven, and I saw a French woman, Stéphanie, struggling to walk away with two big bags. She was about my size, maybe a little smaller than me, and I'd guess she was about fifty. She had short red hair and nice-looking clothes on, and makeup—she didn't look anything like what my idea of a homeless person used to be. I had seen her before at Montesquieu, and she didn't speak any English, but we used to smile at each other.

I carried one of Stéphanie's suitcases for her over to the office above Les Halles where they let a few homeless people leave their stuff. When we got there, she said thank you and gave me a couple of cigarettes, and we smoked one together. I couldn't speak enough French then to really communicate, so we didn't talk much, but when we'd finished the cigarette, she told me, "*Venez avec moi,*" and she took me to the strangest place.

It was deep underground, almost hidden on one of the big avenues that head west at Republic, near the Kentucky Fried Chicken. I know I'd walked past and never knew it was there. We walked down several flights of steps, and there were a lot of immigrant men hanging around the stairway. They stared at us long and hard, but Stéphanie paid no attention.

Way down underground there was a Salvation Army center. I guess it was an old metro station. At least, that's what it looked like. It was this big, tiled space with a desk set up where you signed in, and it was completely crammed with men. Some of them were sleeping in sleeping bags in the corners and others were arguing, drinking coffee, or playing with their phones.

I was not feeling right about this place. It was very depressing, almost scary, but Stéphanie seemed OK, and she showed me there were showers that locked, reserved for women. Then she opened a door in back and there was an actual hair salon for homeless people. I couldn't believe it.

Stéphanie had an appointment to have her hair done for free, and with sign language and pointing, she managed to get across that she thought I should get my hair done too.

The last time I had had my hair done professionally was probably the day I got married. Money was always tight, and to spend it on a salon was a luxury I couldn't afford, so I always used to cut and highlight it myself with stuff I bought from a supermarket.

Since it was free, I made an appointment for next time, which was a month later, and it was pretty funny to think I was going to get a professional haircut now that I was stranded and living on the streets of Paris with no money.

⚜ ⚜ ⚜

Around the middle of December, Suzanne, one of the social workers at Agora, finally agreed to give me an appointment so we could talk about how she could help me out. I needed metro tickets and maybe a meal ticket, and most of all a voucher so I could count on being able to sleep at Montesquieu every night.

She made an appointment with me at Agora for ten in the morning, and when I got there, she was inside the glass office talking on the telephone. I tried to enter the office, and this other lady with blond hair kept turning me away, saying Suzanne was busy. She kept doing this until about eleven. Then I went to use the toilet, and when I came back, there wasn't anyone in the office, and the blond-haired lady had turned the lights out and was locking the door.

I said, *"Excusez-moi, madame, J'ai rendez-vous avec Suzanne"* (Excuse me, ma'am, I have an appointment with Suzanne). But she said very firmly, "Suzanne *fini*, gone."

So the next time I saw Suzanne there on duty, I went to see her and she made another appointment to meet me, this time at the shelter on rue Montesquieu where she also worked, but that time she just never showed up.

The social workers knew they had power over us, and almost all of them seemed to take advantage of that, or they acted like if they kept looking the other way, you'd eventually disappear. They didn't understand that we were there because we sincerely needed their help, not for their amusement. We needed them, especially the women, so we could get off the street and find a place that was safe, instead of walking all night long.

It was so disheartening. There didn't seem to be any way to wake these people up. Our survival was sometimes truly in their hands, and they were social workers. I don't want to believe it's because they don't care, so it must be that they don't understand. I don't know how to get it across.

Maybe every social worker should have to live on the street for a week or two in the winter, as part of their training, like a boot camp. Just throw them out there, and they should have to survive that week with no tickets, no money or resources of any kind, like many of the homeless people on the street have to survive.

Yes, perhaps it sounds a little harsh. But if you ever actually lived on the street with no resources, and the social workers were your hope for survival, and they played games with you like not showing up for appointments repeatedly and acting like they didn't speak your language just so they didn't have to help you, I think you would understand why I suggest this. I truly believe it would make them better social workers. Hopefully they'd develop a little empathy and respect for homeless people if they had to live in their shoes for a little while.

⚜ ⚜ ⚜

Now all I kept with me was one spare pair of underwear, a T-shirt, and socks. I was wearing layers: another T-shirt, a long-underwear shirt, a blouse, and a sweater. I kept one book and any food I had in a plastic bag. It was the guy from Jamaica who told me how important the bags are. One day he saw me over by the Jardin des Halles, and I guess I had some kind of crumpled supermarket bag I found on the street, like a bag from Ed, the discount supermarket. He said, "What are you doing? You can't walk around like that."

He took me down into Les Halles mall and showed me how to go through the garbage there and find a good shopping bag. He told me the brown plastic bags that say FNAC are the best. All the homeless people look for those, because they can hold a ton of stuff without breaking, and they last.

He was right. If you're a woman walking around with a beat-up old plastic bag, wearing lots of layers, and maybe your hair's a little messy, people judge you and treat you differently. They don't respect you. Like if you need directions, they might not bother to answer you.

If you have a good shopping bag, and appear to have it together, you get more respect, and people are more likely to help you, or that was my perception of it, anyway. It was survival tactic. A lot of homeless people in France are disguised as regular people. There are so many facilities where they can bathe and do their laundry for free in the city. In Portland I always felt like you could see or smell a homeless person, but in Paris, you could be talking to one and not even realize it.

It's so difficult for the homeless women. Some of the ones who had been on the street six months or more would seem to drift off to their own reality. Reality is based on the observer, and it's like they'd create a reality they could live with and just stay inside that world a lot of the time.

I'm guessing makeup goes first, then maybe clean clothes, and if you don't keep so clean, there's a homeless smell. The women who really lived in their own reality seemed to go through spells of not taking care of themselves: Sometimes they didn't bathe or change their clothes, and most of the social workers didn't even know how to reach them.

Then occasionally something seemed to click, and they would be freshly bathed, with clean clothes and makeup on. Everyone was talking to them again, and other homeless men and women were offering them resources again. It was always good to have them back, if only temporarily.

But there was one woman that was really out there in her own reality all the time, and one day a social worker got her into a women's shelter. The change was unbelievable. She started functioning again, bathing, wearing clean clothes, and taking part in coherent conversations. I didn't even realize it was her at first; she just came up and started talking to me, and as I was introducing myself, I recognized her.

She appeared to have completely turned herself around, once she was in a safe environment. That made me wonder how many of the men and women out there could be saved, if they were only given a legitimate chance.

It also made me wonder how many regular people could handle being homeless, how long would it take after being brought out of your safe environment before you started to lose it? If you suddenly lost your home and had to walk all night to avoid being attacked, and the social workers either ignored you or judged you because of your situation or the country you were born in, if you were treated like you were bad or crazy every day over a period of time, how long would it take before you started acting like everyone treated you?

⚜ ⚜ ⚜

It was really cold outside all the time now. Everyone kept saying this was the worst winter Paris had seen in a long time. So if I couldn't get into Montesquieu, the nights were bitter. I really needed help, because I couldn't take much more.

⚜ ⚜ ⚜

Men offered me money for a hand job all the time. Maybe some women take them up on it. I'm not judging that; I understand the need to survive, and I know what it's like to be hungry. It's probably the reason there are so few homeless women: The risks are so high. It's very dangerous and difficult to keep warm and stay alive, but I never considered it. I've been with four men my whole life and I was always emotionally involved.

I remember, early one morning, I was looking for a church where someone told me you could get a free breakfast on Sunday.

The street was Saint something. The street was really long, and it was early in the morning, but I could see prostitutes standing outside all the video stores. I had to laugh out loud, that many sex shops and people selling sex on a street named Saint something.

And I had no idea women with curves were so popular in Europe. The French and Arab men seem to be particularly fond of them, and that came as quite a shock to me. You see, in America, men are obsessed with physical form too, but most of them want very thin Barbie doll–type women. At first I thought they were joking with me, when they would walk by and give me two thumbs up, but apparently not.

These men are not to be confused with the wolves. There are many regular men in France that flirt with women, but when a woman says no, they leave her alone.

But the wolves—their favorite type appears to be blond-haired, English-speaking women with at least some curves. They are also attracted to certain behaviors. I recently learned that smoking gets their attention right away, and of course I stopped as soon as I learned that.

They also look at the way you dress, and if you're wearing a headscarf or a hijab, it seems like they leave you alone. Unfortunately, I didn't learn all of that until after I got off the street. I wish I'd figured it out earlier.

Late one weekend, around midnight, when I hadn't eaten much of anything, Agora was closed, and I couldn't get into Montesquieu, I walked past an Italian restaurant. There were still a few people eating inside, and I couldn't help staring at the food on their plates through the window as I walked by.

A man—I guess maybe an Italian—came to the door and yelled out, "Are you hungry, *tu as faim*?"

I kept walking, but I said, "I'm OK, *ça va*."

He asked in English, "Are you sure? We're getting ready to close and I'll be throwing food out."

I hesitated, but my stomach was growling, really yelling, and I had to walk for the rest of the night. So I walked back to the restaurant. The deal seemed safe: There were still some people inside eating.

The man asked what I wanted to drink and I said just water, but he brought me a glass of red wine. He said, "It will warm you up, it's very cold outside."

I asked again for a glass of water. While he was in the back, I looked around, and there was a little bar with a sink, so I washed my hands and filled a glass with water. He came back with a big plate of food and all of a sudden, when I saw the look on his face, I didn't feel hungry anymore. I felt sick.

I asked for the toilet and he showed me one downstairs. There were still two tables with customers at them when I went down there. Once I'd locked myself in the toilet, I just sat down and I started feeling better. I was gone five or maybe ten minutes.

When I was back upstairs, the man was walking two thin, dark-skinned men to the door—they looked like his employees. I sat down and he locked the door after them, and then I realized the other customers were gone, and we were the only two people in the restaurant, but now I was locked inside.

I kept telling myself not to panic, that I must remain present. I told myself over and over again, and I focused on trying to slow down my heart, which was pounding.

The man kept telling me, "Eat, eat, it tastes better when it's warm." So I tried to take a few bites of food and drink the water. He was standing between me and the bar, I was feeling really ill again, and I asked if I could leave and take the food with me. I lied and said I was meeting someone at the Hôtel de Ville and they'd be worried if I was any later, but he just kept clicking at a computer that was sitting on the counter and ignored me.

I had to get him to willingly open the door, but how?

He asked if I knew anything about computers, and I said, "Not much." He told me his computer was stuck and asked me to take a look at it. I told him again that I didn't know much about computers, but he insisted I take a look. He said he was sure I could help him.

I walked over and he had hard-core porn playing on the computer. He asked, "Do you like this?"

I kept telling myself to remain present, most of all not to react. I stood silent, as he started unzipping his pants.

I felt sick again. I rushed to the sink at the little bar and I vomited, and then washed my face and mouth, and when I looked up, he was gone, but I was still locked inside.

After a few minutes he reappeared from a back room with my food in a to-go container. He handed it to me, walked to the door, and unlocked it. He said, "Just go."

I rushed out the door and turned around, and I sincerely thanked him.

⚜ ⚜ ⚜

Thomas introduced me to a homeless woman from Czechoslovakia. Her name was Johanna, but I ended up calling her Chex. She had a mess of sandy blond hair, and she wore men's sneakers and blue jeans, with a black-and-white scarf rolled up and tied around her forehead like a bandana. Even though it was the middle of December, she looked hot—she had her T-shirt sleeves rolled up and you could see her powerful arms and shoulders.

She gave me a black vinyl purse and showed me all the little pockets, then sat back beaming. I was embarrassed. I told Thomas I liked the purse but I didn't have any money to pay for it, but Chex said, "No—present, it's a present for you." Maybe one of the social workers at Montesquieu gave it to her. Women were always bringing in their old stuff so they could give to people in need. I liked Chex immediately; she was a little eccentric, but there was just something very real and kind about her eyes.

That night while I was walking I found a yellow rose on the ground and immediately thought of her. I don't know about other countries, but in America, yellow roses mean friendship. I picked it up to give to her the next morning, but I couldn't find her, so I ended up giving it to Thomas.

I had trouble understanding Chex at first. Her English wasn't great, and her native tongue was German, but there are many different ways to communicate other than speaking. The more we hung out, the better we became at reading each other's expressions, signals, and body language. Chex said she'd been living on the street in Paris since August, and before that, it was hard to figure out where she'd lived. She said she loved Switzerland and had been in Italy, Germany, all over the place.

I ask her where she slept, and she said, "On the sidewalk."

"How do you manage that?" I asked. I had to walk all night or the wolves would get me. Sometimes I had to fight them off even while I was walking. Chex knew what I meant, but she said she had a safe place where nobody bothered her.

I was exhausted, and I wanted to know what a safe place for a woman on the street looked like. I kept asking Chex to show me her safe place, so she finally agreed to share it with me for one night.

We walked through Les Halles park and came to a big old circular building that I'd often noticed. There were two tents set up under the curved archways, a normal-sized one and a small one, and I guess someone was in the larger one, because it was very cold outside. The smaller one was navy blue and it had a little zipper door with a padlock. Chex pulled out a key and unlocked it. This was her safe place.

When you have a tent to sleep in, people don't bother you so much. They don't know who is inside, whether you're a man or a woman, so they stay away. You're still on the street, but you're almost safe.

There wasn't much room, because Chex had several plastic bags, plus a sleeping bag and a blanket, and some bottles of water and food. But it was really convenient. There was even a magic toilet in sight, where you could wash up.

Chex said there were rules for the tent:

1. *No boots or shoes inside the tent.*

2. *No eating inside the tent.*

3. *No drinking inside the tent.*

4. *No smoking inside the tent.*

Then she disappeared for a moment and came back with a large white comforter that was hidden in some boxes by the circular building. She said she'd loaned it to a friend the night before and he had left it there for her.

By the time we'd both climbed inside with her things and my two bags, there wasn't much room left, and as we struggled to get into our sleeping bags, the tent bulged every time we moved. Once we were finally zipped up, we heard voices outside, and Chex scrambled out of her sleeping bag as quick as she could and raced to unlock the padlock from the zipper door.

"What's wrong?" I asked.

"Nothing," Chex said. She was smiling from ear to ear. "It's the people from the church." Once or twice a week, two people from a local church brought coffee and soup, and sometimes even sandwiches, to the people they knew lived in tents in the neighborhood.

It was very cold and they were very kind. We sat inside the tent, as close to the door as we could get, and ate a sandwich. Then we drank creamy chicken Cup-a-Soup and coffee and smoked a cigarette. So much for rules two, three, and four. There was a French woman named Katharine who had a tent set up right next to Chex. She looked to be in her sixties, although it's hard to tell. She wasn't a stable person at all, plus she smoked a lot of hashish, and she was pretty out of it that night, but everything was OK.

We got back into our sleeping bags, and Chex fluffed up the big white down comforter the best she could. It seemed like every inch of the tent was so full it would explode. We both burst out laughing, and I told her this is what it must feel like to be packed in a box with those little white foam pieces. Chex tucked me in, we laughed some more, and then said goodnight.

The small tent kept our body heat in—it was almost too warm, and I had to push the white comforter off, but it was one of the best nights of sleep I'd had in a long time.

It was cold and wet the next morning, and Chex seemed frustrated. She wasn't real sociable first thing in the morning, before she'd had coffee and a cigarette. She told me I would have to get my own tent because hers was too small.

I saw her point, it was small, but I felt like I'd really connected with Chex. We couldn't really sit down and talk about our life stories, but she was really kind and had a warm heart.

There were other people at Agora I felt safe and friendly with too. We were all kind of in the same situation, trying to get in to see a social worker, and trying to find a decent place to rest. We all had problems, it wasn't just me.

⚜ ⚜ ⚜

After leaving Chex's tent, I went to take a shower at the free place near the Centre Pompidou. I didn't like to use the showers at Agora, because there was a peephole in the wall, and at Montesquieu men would push the door open to the women's shower room, like they were making a mistake and just blundered into the wrong place.

The Centre Pompidou is a funny building—it's both a library and a museum—and it always looked to me like a giant hamster cage, the kind with all the hard plastic tubes that the hamster gets to run around in. You can go inside there and walk around if you have money to spend, but I didn't, so if the weather was OK I would sit outside and watch musicians and mimes fooling around for the tourists.

That morning after I slept in Chex's tent, I was sitting there on a bench, and I met a doctor from Texas. I guess he could tell I was American—he came up and asked if I knew where a pharmacy was.

I told him, "Just look for a green cross, they're all over the place," and it's true, you never saw such a city as Paris for pharmacies. But he said he'd done that and he couldn't find Tylenol anywhere. He really needed Tylenol, because it was the only thing that would relieve his headaches.

A guy came up to us, begging for money, and I told him, "*No euros, no travail pour l'instant, desole*" (no money, no work for the moment, sorry), which was about all I could manage to say at that time, but it got the message across.

The doctor said, "My daughter lived here a while back, and she says the best thing to do with all the homeless people is to just ignore them."

Looking back on it, it was pretty funny, because I don't think he ever realized he was sitting there talking to a homeless woman. I told him that in Paris, homeless people are very cleverly disguised. There are free showers and places they can stow their bags. You would never realize how many homeless people there truly are.

8

La Soupe Saint-Eustache

Thomas told me he wanted to go back to the United Kingdom for Christmas. He had friends he could stay with for the holidays, and he missed being around people who spoke English. But he was worried about leaving, because he had almost made it through ninety days and was hoping he could start getting a check every month and find a room to rent, and if he left the country it might mess that up.

Finally, after his sleeping bag was stolen one weekend, he decided to go anyway, and I knew it was better for him. At least he would be off the streets for Christmas. And it's not like I really missed him a whole lot. Thomas was just a friendly face I ran into sometimes at Agora, but I felt much more alone when he was gone.

That Sunday night I was hungry, so I went back to the soup line he'd shown me at Gare de l'Est, but I was on my own. I was one of very few women in the crowd waiting for the vans to drive up. I hadn't noticed how few women there were when I was there with Thomas. He had said that by a quarter to eight there would be two or three vans with food, but that night there were none.

A group of men walked up and started talking to me, and they said there wouldn't be any food tonight. They were from Afghanistan, and at first I didn't perceive them as dangerous, which was weird; I had developed a kind of sixth sense for wolves, which I believe saved me more than once. At first these men didn't seem to be wolves. They seemed respectful and well educated, and they spoke good English. Still, there were a number of them, five or six, and nobody else around who would have cared if anything had happened to me.

They introduced themselves and said they had an apartment close by, with some canned food and a heater. They invited me to come home with them, to get warm and eat.

They asked where I slept, and I lied and told them Montesquieu, but they seemed to know I was lying. I wondered if they had seen me walking all night, and then one of them told me I could spend the night at their apartment. "Just sex with him and with me," he said, pointing at another guy, "and then sleep all night long, no problem."

I said no and started moving away fast, but they kept following me and said, "What's the problem? You're American, right? That means you love sex, we know that." I was slowly discovering this shocking stereotype, mainly of the Middle-Eastern mentality. I was scared. Why hadn't I felt their wolf presence before? Was I that exhausted?

I told them I was meeting a girlfriend at ten, and that sometimes she let me sleep on the couch at her place. I focused on my breathing—I knew I needed to be fully present. I told them I had to go, and that if I didn't meet her at Châtelet, she'd be worried.

They smiled and moved closer and one of them said, "Aren't you going to the shelter at Montesquieu?"

I said, "My friend has a boyfriend. When he's out of town, she lets me sleep over, but when he's in Paris, I sleep at Montesquieu. But he's not here now, and if I don't get there, she'll look for me, she knew I was going to the soup line at Gare de l'Est . . ." I was babbling.

They asked why I wasn't eating with her, then. I said her boyfriend was leaving at nine thirty that night, and anyway I didn't like to eat her food, because I had no money to give her for expenses. I was almost at the subway entrance, around the corner of the road.

They looked at each other, and the same guy said, "OK, no problem. We're always here around Gare de l'Est," and that it was a standing offer. If my girlfriend didn't show up, or another night, if I got too cold or hungry, I should come back there and find them. He was still polite.

And then they let me go, and I felt a flood of relief.

I bummed a metro ticket and jumped on the next subway, and as I was sitting safely on the train, I thought how lucky I was. If we were in America, they might have pulled a gun on me and dragged me into an alley. I felt grateful to them—it sounds crazy, but they were pleasant and professional. They said, 'This is what we have to offer you and this is what we want in exchange," and then they let me go. I kind of had to respect that.

But I was still hungry, and there was nowhere I could go for food now, so I went back to the Louvre and I kept walking.

At about five in the morning I was finished, spent, no more. There was a construction site set up in the corner of one of the long arms around the courtyard, with metal barriers and part of a wooden fence to separate it from the sidewalk. It didn't look exactly safe, but I figured I could hide behind the fence till daybreak; it was about five when I curled up in a shadow.

I thought I would be OK there till the sun rose, but I was wrong. I felt hands on my shoulders, and when I lifted my head, the wolf had grabbed a handful of my hair. Another hand came down on my crotch; I had a small hole in my black Lee jeans, on the inner thigh, where they were worn from walking so much. I pulled away, but his fingers found the hole and I heard my jeans ripping. He was physically ripping my jeans off my body. At first I pulled away, but the more I resisted, the stronger he seemed to become.

Suddenly, my mind became still, almost as if it were happening in slow motion, and I stopped resisting. I leaned into him, and it knocked him off balance, so he had to let go of me for a moment to keep from toppling over. I was able to scramble out of his grasp and run away.

I went to the police station nearby to report I had been attacked, but they said no English. "This is France, we speak French." I pulled back my coat and showed them what was left of my pants and the claw marks the wolf had made on my thigh. But the policeman kept saying, "This is France, you must speak French—*Parlez-vous français?*" and they were saying everything in French, so I believed they honestly couldn't understand me.

I left overcome with emotion. Once I was able to let the emotions go and put some space between them and the moment, I realized I was OK. It wasn't the end of the world, I just needed a pair of pants.

Thomas had told me about an office on Rambuteau where a nonprofit organization had given him a warm coat. It was close by and he said they always had piles of clothes behind the counter. So when they opened at nine in the morning, I went there and asked them for a pair of pants. There were two big piles of jeans behind the counter, and the woman spoke English as she said, "You must have a ticket to get a pair of pants."

So I asked for a ticket, and she left and came back and handed me a square piece of paper with an address and a metro station typed out on it. I took it, and began lining up with the other people for clothes, but the woman still wouldn't give me any. She said, "You can't get in this line, these are men's clothes. You must go across town to the address on the ticket."

I opened up my coat again and showed her what was left of my pants. I told her I'd been attacked early that morning and I needed a pair of pants because mine were ripped apart.

She said, "These clothes are for men only."

I said I didn't care, but she kept telling me I needed to go way across town to the address on the ticket she'd given me. I kept opening my coat and showing her. I couldn't bear to go across town with barely no pants on, but she insisted I had no choice, and she refused give me a pair of pants from the pile behind the counter.

I made my way across town as people stared. They looked astonished, and a few pointed their fingers at me and laughed—walking around Paris with practically no pants on. I finally found the address on the ticket, and the place was closed.

⚜ ⚜ ⚜

In spite of all the emotional turmoil, my stomach wouldn't stop growling and cramping with hunger pains, so I knew I had to find something to eat. Before Thomas left, he suggested I try to get a meal ticket at an office run by the Restaurants du Coeur, which is like a homeless restaurant service. It was across the way from the office with the clothes in Les Halles, which is a big shopping mall right downtown. I had gone there the Friday before, and the men who worked there said they had no meal tickets, but one of the guys was from England and he knew the supervisor of their restaurant at metro station Chevaleret. He called her, and she agreed to let me eat lunch there every weekday, even if I didn't have a meal voucher.

So I'd been there the previous Friday. It was down an alley just near the metro station, like a series of prefabs set up in an empty lot. It was very temporary looking and there was a sign up toward the end of the alley, so it's not like I could see it from the street, but there was a crowd of people waiting. And it worked—the supervisor, Christine, let me in, and I got some hot food: a bowl of lentils with a small hot dog in them. She even gave me a woolen hat, which I really needed. That was nice.

So that Monday, with just about no pants left, I went there—to the Restaurant du Coeur at a metro station that sounded like Chevrolet. I tried to explain the arrangement to the woman checking tickets because she wouldn't even let me get in line without one. She sent me to talk to the supervisor, only this time it wasn't Christine. There was another lady in charge. She spoke English, and I was so relieved at that—I thought it meant I'd be able to eat.

I explained again about the arrangement with Christine, but she raised her voice and said very firmly in English, "You don't speak French, you don't eat! This is France, you must speak French!"

I explained, "I didn't choose to be here, I got stuck here."

I pulled my coat back and showed her what was left of my jeans. I explained I was attacked and I hadn't eaten much since lunchtime Friday—it was almost impossible to find food on a weekend without a meal ticket—and by now it was Monday afternoon. I had walked all weekend till I gave out at five that morning. Every time I stopped, the wolves would try to attack.

I told her I was hungry and the cramps and growling in my stomach wouldn't stop. But she kept raising her voice louder and louder until she was yelling and repeating the phrase in English:

"You don't speak French, you don't eat." She was completely delirious.

I couldn't hold them back: The tears started flowing and wouldn't stop. There was all of this food around us and she refused to give me any. I started raising my voice.

"When dealing with unconsciousness, it is easy to get drawn down into the unconsciousness."

I repeated, "I didn't choose to be here, I am stuck here." I said, "Do you honestly think I'd move to a foreign country where I don't speak the language? Look what your country has done to me, what your men have done to me." I showed her my bare leg with the claw mark the wolf had left behind.

She yelled even louder, "You don't speak French, you don't eat."

There were two pitchers of milk on the counter between us, and before I knew what I was doing, I was shoving them over, aiming for her. A man jumped in front of her and the pitchers fell onto him instead, and then another man gently took my arm and escorted me out the door.

⚜ ⚜ ⚜

So there I was, legs barely covered, stomach in cramps, severe pain in my feet and legs, and exhausted from all the walking.

At that moment, I gave up. I found a bench nearby, and I just sat there in the cold. I was in a state of shock. The tears eventually stopped, and I felt numb.

When I sat down, they were serving lunch at the homeless restaurant, and the next time I looked up, it was getting dark, so I guess it was four or five hours later. Days of walking without food or sleep, bogus addresses to get pants across town, nobody who would help me—I just blanked, I temporarily checked out.

I vaguely remember some passerby told me to go to the big church on Rambuteau. I never even looked up to see who it was. He said there was a soup line there, and you didn't need a ticket.

I made my way back across town from Chevaleret to Rambuteau. I was frozen, exhausted, and in a lot of pain, so at first I didn't think I could walk all that way. I just kept telling myself to focus on each step as I was taking it, one foot in front of the other. When I got near the church, I remembered I had some alcohol disinfectant in my coat pocket that I'd brought with me from America, so I tried to clean up. I dabbed it onto my leg with the sleeve of my black sweater, then I put some on my hands and cleaned them, and I walked around to the front of the church.

There was a table with a huge pot of soup on it out in front, and they were scraping out the last of the soup.

The tears started flowing again. Some of the volunteers came up to me: a woman with short blond hair in her early fifties, a balding gentleman, and a small woman with shoulder-length dark hair.

They said, "It's OK, we have more," but I just couldn't seem to stop crying. I was broken, and in an unimaginable amount of pain.

I had hit rock bottom.

I showed the volunteers my leg, and they took me inside and let me sit down. They brought me food and water and a blanket.

While sitting there at La Soupe Saint-Eustache, with these wonderful people taking care of me, I began to realize I was resisting everything: being stuck in a foreign country, not speaking the language, having no money, having no place to stay, having no food, the social workers' refusal to help, that I couldn't even get into Montesquieu. It was at that moment that I started gaining awareness. I told them I was a good person in a bad situation. I had a moment of clarity, and I stopped identifying with my life situation.

They asked me where I slept, and I said, "If I don't get into Montesquieu, I can't sleep. I walk all night to keep the wolves from attacking me."

I pulled back my coat again and said, "This is what happens when I stop walking."

They said, "Haven't you called 115?" and I said that yes, I always did, every day, but they'd already told me they didn't have a bed for me tonight.

"Where else can you sleep?" they asked.

I told them I had slept one night in Chex's tent across the Jardin des Halles, but it was too small. Still, they walked me over there— we were only about two hundred yards from where she slept—and she said no again. She showed them: There really wasn't enough room in her tiny tent, with all her bags.

They asked me if I would agree to go to the police station; they said maybe the police could help me get into Montesquieu for the night. I explained that I didn't speak enough French and the police didn't understand me, but the volunteers said they would translate. They took me there, and told me that the police agreed that if it was an emergency, and if 115 really couldn't give me a bed, I could even sleep at the police station.

I thanked them and told them to go home. It was late, and I figured I would be fine. And I was: A policewoman called 115—they have a special line to get through in case of emergencies—and 115 called Montesquieu, and they agreed to let me in for the night on an emergency basis.

⚜ ⚜ ⚜

It was such a relief to be at Montesquieu among familiar faces. It was crowded because it was so cold outside, and all of the beds and most of the chairs were taken, so I would be sleeping on one of the cots. I took a deep breath and surrendered to the fact that I would have to sleep with men on either side of me, with barely any pants left.

The guy from Jamaica was there and he asked how I got in— he'd already seen me being turned away a couple of times from Montesquieu because I had no ticket. I pulled back my coat and showed him the wolf's claw marks. I hoped if the others realized I'd been attacked, they would leave me alone and let me rest.

In the morning, Mohamed was the worker on duty. He was great: Whenever he was working at the door at Montesquieu, I knew he'd let me in. He was just a real nice guy. He was shooing us all out into the rain after breakfast, and he said, "Call 115 right away, make sure you get them early and you'll get another bed here for tonight."

I explained that I called 115 just about every day, and I always got the runaround—no bed, American tourist.

But Mohamed said that wasn't right. He really seemed to know how the system worked, and he told me it wasn't true. He said that 115 was for anyone who was homeless, it didn't matter what country you were born in, and if they told you no, you could demand to speak to a supervisor. He told me how to say it in French, and to tell the supervisor that I knew 115 wasn't only for French people.

When Mohamed said that—"One one five is for all homeless people"—I remember feeling a jolt of surprise and pain, and then thinking, *He's right, that's what I am.*

I'm a homeless person.

I had no control, and I was totally adrift with no money, no ticket for a shelter, and no way home. I was just a homeless person on the street in a foreign country where I didn't speak the language, with no idea how to get out of this jam.

I called 115 as usual. I waited on hold for a long time to get someone who spoke English, and then she came on and told me, "Not for you, American tourist," and went through the whole spiel.

I told her what Mohamed had said, and she told me to hold on while she asked her supervisor.

She was gone for almost a half hour, and when she came back, she apologized for taking so long. She said, "My supervisor had to research it because we don't get many Americans calling us, but you're right. You are supposed to call 115 even if you're American, and after you've been here for three months, you'll have even more rights," and she told me I could go back to Montesquieu that night.

That was a relief, and then I went to Agora for coffee in what was left of my pants, and I asked a social worker for a new pair. She gave me a ticket with an address that looked like the same place I'd gone to the day before, so I threw it in the trash.

Then Chex came in and I asked her if she knew where I could get a pair of pants. She said, "Sometimes they have extra clothes locked up in the social workers' closet at Montesquieu—you should check there at two, when they open for the women's group."

I said, "What women's group?" and Chex explained that Sabrina, one of social workers at Montesquieu, used to open the main room for women from two to five in the afternoon, Monday through Friday, no wolves allowed.

When I walked in, the atmosphere was kind of depressing. There were maybe a dozen women—I saw a woman named Mathilde and a couple of other women I recognized. Most of them were resting, with their legs propped up on chairs, and nobody was talking—it wasn't the picture I came up with when I thought "women's group."

But there was tea and sometimes something to eat, and when I took off my coat and said what had happened, the social worker,

Sabrina, found a pair of pants locked in a back room. So about thirty-three hours after I was attacked and sent all over town on what appeared to be a cruel scavenger hunt, I finally had a pair of pants.

⚜ ⚜ ⚜

I went back to La Soupe Saint-Eustache for food that night, and almost every night after that. There was always something hot to eat, coffee, dessert, and sometimes salad, and they gave me a bag to take away too, with bread and something nonperishable I could eat for lunch the next day.

They were good people, the volunteers in that soup line. I felt a real connection with them. It must be a very special community they have. There were probably two or three hundred homeless people there every night, and I guess the volunteers probably worked all day to prepare the food. But they were always very kind and respectful; they never sneered or judged or joked about you, or gave you a hard time because of the country you were born in. It seemed like they sincerely wanted to help.

The attitude of most of the workers at Agora was basically, "You're homeless and I'm not, and I decide if you get to go to the toilet." They judged us; they acted like they were different from us, superior because their life situation was more stable than ours, and some of them really appeared to enjoy playing games with us. It was basically all about power and control.

But at Saint-Eustache the volunteers seemed to function at a different level of consciousness. They always greeted everyone with a smile, and seemed really happy to see you. They didn't judge anyone because of their life situation, and they seemed to understand on some level, we're all the same. Their mentality was "How can we be of service to you?"

9

Moment of Surrender

I was rereading *A New Earth* in a kind of slow, long loop. Sometimes I would close the book after just a sentence or a paragraph. I would sit on an icy bench in the Jardin des Halles or by the river watching flakes of snow rest on the cobblestones for a moment before they melted; I would close my eyes and focus on my breathing, and when I opened them, I felt more connected to the world.

I began trying to focus part of my awareness much of the time on my breathing and the pace of my legs as I walked, seeing how they fell into cadence together. There's a lot going on when you're walking, a lot to pay attention to. There's traffic and people walking past, the looks on their faces. You pay different kinds of attention: sometimes you're minding things just enough so that you don't knock into stuff, and sometimes you're really lingering on it all—the buses, the motorcycles swarming everywhere, the different noises, how distinct they are.

But after a while you notice it all starts to look and sound the same.

There's another stage: you're not really paying any kind of attention at all to the world around you. You're just focused on the movement. The car noise has died down and you're not walking anywhere, just staying on the move. You're not frightened anymore, and there aren't any wolves around, although probably if you rest for a while one will come up.

You've got a nice, slow, steady pace going, and you feel the way the weight falls down onto the bones of your foot, but you're not wincing anymore—that's just extra energy. You're accepting the pain when it comes, you feel the impact of ground all the way up to your knees and hips, but you keep moving. You're not staring at anything, or getting caught up in what's going around you, and your mind is quiet.

You put one foot in front of the other: That's all it takes.

❖ ❖ ❖

"Everything that happens is part of the greater whole and its purpose. The present moment is not an obstacle to be overcome."

I began to try to stop blaming the social workers and all the other people for not helping me. I tried to see it from a different perspective; perhaps they were doing me a favor by showing me that I *could* do it.

I tried to stop worrying all the time. There comes a point when you have to focus all your energy on staying awake, minding your surroundings, and being aware of who is close by. You're alert, but you don't worry about every little thing. They have a saying in Tibet: "If the problem can be solved, there's no use worrying about it, and if it can't be solved, worrying will do no good."

Of course, I was aware that if there was a suspicious person following me, then I needed to find a place with people and lights and get there as fast as possible. But I began to stop expecting other people to make me safe, feed me, or get me "home."

I didn't give up. I gave in to what was happening to me, and I tried to stop resisting everything—being hungry, homeless, and broke. And when the mental clouds dispersed, and I started accepting that I was on my own, and I would have to work it out, things just seemed to start falling into place. A lot of my self-created suffering began to fall away: the anxious, stressful, negative thinking, wanting, fear, anticipation, and blame. I guess I'd begun to figure out how things worked, too, and I'd started understanding a little French. That was part of it, but I also suddenly started being at the right place at the right time.

⚜ ⚜ ⚜

There was the women's group at Montesquieu in the afternoons, Monday through Friday. They'd let you come in out of the weather from two to five, and you could just sit in the main room and drink coffee or tea and maybe eat something, in a warm place with no wolves.

I guess they knew it was hard for the women, but sometimes the atmosphere could get pretty rocky, if Mathilde was having a tantrum. There was also an Indian woman who had a real short fuse, and she could get really violent, so Sabrina would often give her a metro ticket and send her across town to Halte-Femmes, another daytime shelter for women, but most of them were very unstable.

Another social worker said she was going to start a French class at Montesquieu every Friday. That was cool. A few things were really beginning to make sense to me in French, and I wanted to work on that.

But the class was always being interrupted, and if there was anything else going on, like if the phone rang or one of the unstable women started yelling, then the social worker had to deal with that instead. Some days the other women just wouldn't show up, and class would be canceled, or she would leave after her other work was finished, before teaching class, and it could be a little frustrating.

But if I resisted, it only made it worse, so I used these situations to practice gaining awareness of when I was resisting. Just because I was becoming aware of it didn't mean I was able to stop doing it immediately, but I realized the more I resisted, the more pain I felt. And whenever I was able to accept the situations I was in—even if only temporarily—and not identify with them, the pain started to melt away.

"Surrender to what is. Say 'Yes' to life, and see how life suddenly starts working for you rather than against you."

I also knew I could get food at Saint-Eustache every night and have the little sack for lunch the next day, and they always greeted everyone with a smile.

And there was also the Salvation Army place. I went back there for my hair appointment, and it was pretty surreal. The tunnel was really dingy, but the woman who colored my hair was so gentle and professional—she was really nice. She showed me the box of hair dye before she used it, so I could check that the color was right, and she even massaged my scalp for a few minutes. It felt great.

Afterwards she told me I should come back at six because they were going to have a Christmas party. I was thinking, *OK, maybe there'll be some soda pop, food, and Christmas music.* I've always loved Christmas music, especially gospel, and when I was a kid, "Frosty the Snowman" was my favorite song. In America there's an animated TV special about Frosty they show every year around Christmastime.

I wondered if that would be different in France, so I hung around Republic and went back there, but it was just nothing. They had a little bit of music and a few sandwiches eventually, but nobody was happy or celebrating in any way.

So I sat down and really paid attention to the men there. I even asked some of them where they were from, and the greatest percent was from Afghanistan and Pakistan. As I gazed around the room I wondered how many of these men where homeless and stuck in a foreign country as a result of the mindless war America had been a large part of.

I had always been against the war. It was one thing to see it on TV, but if you have any empathy or compassion, when you're sitting in a room surrounded by refugees, it forces you to a whole new level of consciousness. My perception of America had suddenly shifted.

I wanted to help them, but I wasn't in a position to help anyone. So I headed out, and there was a guy on the stairs playing his guitar. As I walked by, he started playing Nirvana, so I sat and listened, and a few other guys gathered around and joined in.

It was entertaining for a while, and then I walked back to Agora. Suzanne was getting women together to form a choir and sing Christmas songs. I knew at least three of the women were living on the street, and I thought it was more important to find these women a safe, warm place to sleep, but Suzanne was researching songs they could sing on YouTube.

Suzanne wanted me to sing too. The weather was wet and cold, and I was really exhausted from all the walking, so I made a joke about it. I said, "Suzanne, I can't sing today, I don't have my Mickey Mouse ears."

The next day I was standing outside Agora when Francois, Salim's friend, came by, and he suggested we take a stroll in the Jardin des Halles. He was always kind and respectful, and there wasn't any harm in that, so I went along. His English was OK. It was almost like he had been working on it. At six he said, "Come on, it's time to eat."

But we were headed back to Agora. I said, "Where are we eating?"

"Here!" he said, and he showed me, in the basement of Agora, way downstairs and along a corridor that's so long you could be in another building, they serve food every night for one euro. You didn't need any kind of meal ticket, and the food was hot, and there was plenty of it. Nobody had ever told me, and there were no signs up, not even in French.

When we got back upstairs, there was a thin man in his early forties sitting at a table. He said he was French, but he spoke some English. He wore a three-piece suit, and had short, dark, curly hair. If you ran into him on the street, you would never guess he was homeless. He saw the bread sticking out of my bag and said,

"Where did you get the bread? Do they have food here?"

I explained that for one euro you could eat dinner downstairs, but I didn't think he had one euro. He was so thin that he looked like he really could be starving to death, so I gave him the rest of my bread and the pâté that I'd saved from dinner for later.

I kept asking myself, why don't they have a sign up or communicate that you can buy a full dinner downstairs for one euro? He was French, and he didn't even know.

⚜ ⚜ ⚜

Chex had told me I should try to get my own tent, and it sounded like a brilliant idea. Her tent was warm and, most of all, pretty safe. After being on the street and having to walk all night, a nice warm little tent looked like a two-star hotel.

Sure, it's just a piece of cloth that separates you from the smell and noise and the people on the sidewalk, but it appeared to work. They didn't know who was inside, so they left you alone. If I found a tent, maybe I could rest long enough to figure something else out.

Someone told me I should go to the office at Les Halles and ask for a tent. They said a doctor from Médecins du Monde was there at certain times of the day, once or twice a week, and he might be able to help. The doctor wasn't there, and the place was just closing, but they gave me the address of a Red Cross store near Place Voltaire.

I walked back to Agora and asked the social workers if I could leave my bags in the office while I walked over there, because it was a pretty long walk, but they refused.

They really didn't care, and I told them, "You really don't care if we die out there." I had no shelter, no sleeping bag or tent—it was really cold outside now—and I just needed to leave my bag there for two hours, but they just kept saying no.

One of the women decided to speak a little English. She said I could go over to the office at Les Halles and apply for a place to leave my bags, but it would take a couple of weeks, and they were closed now.

So Chex took my stuff to her tent. It wasn't that much, but I was hoping to find a tent and a sleeping bag. Then I walked over to Place Voltaire, and found the Red Cross address. Actually, it was just a thrift shop that sold secondhand clothes and books and stuff. I had my American Red Cross ID—I was a volunteer in America— and I showed it to the woman at the cash register and I told her how I'd gotten stuck, and that I didn't have any money or a place to stay.

She went in a back room and came out with a sleeping bag. She told me they didn't have any tents, but she could give me this. It wasn't a new bag, but it wasn't beat up, either, and she just gave it to me for free, and never expected anything in return.

I love the Red Cross. They can be really amazing.

I thanked her, and as I walked back to Agora, I thought it was great to have a sleeping bag, but kind of useless without a tent to sleep in. I knew Francois was the problem solver at Agora, because whenever the men had a problem or needed something they couldn't find, they always went to Francois. He was a nice guy, so I decided to ask him to help me find a tent.

At first he said no, and he seemed really shocked that I would want to sleep on the sidewalk in a tent. He said, "It's too cold, you'll freeze to death," but I explained how I slept in Chex's tent and how warm it was and that it was much safer than walking all night by myself. I told him I was so exhausted and didn't know how much longer I could continue to walk.

He asked, "A tent is *good*?" I said, "Yes, a small one is good, because it keeps your body heat in." It surprised him, but once he thought about it, he agreed to help me.

Francois showed me a little book of places where homeless people could go for help. There were domiciles and places you could wash your clothes, bathe, and leave your stuff. There were many homeless restaurants you could eat at *if* you had a ticket, and doctors you could go to. Having experienced a few domicile places myself, I wasn't sure how this stuff would pan out in reality, but it looked impressive, so I figured it was worth a try.

He told me I should go to a place run by Secours Catholique, near Gare de l'Est. He said I must go early in the morning. When I asked him for directions, he wrote something on a piece of paper in French, and I didn't understand, so I asked if he could take me there.

But he said he was taking his son to Euro Disney, so he would be out of town all day tomorrow. He told me he didn't live with his son anymore, but he looked forward to the days he could visit him. It must have been hard to save up the money to do that—I knew Francois didn't have a place to live, because I saw him at Montesquieu every night I tried to get in.

I walked all around the train station, and looked pretty much all day for Secours Catholique, but I couldn't find it. I asked about fifteen people, but nobody knew where it was, so when it started getting dark, I went back to Agora.

10

The Kind French Man

Suzanne was there at Agora and I asked her, "Can you help me get hold of a tent?"

Suzanne answered, "Oh, but a tent's not the answer for you. I've been seeing you around here for a while now, and I just thought you had a place to stay. We should make an appointment."

"But you already gave me two appointments where you didn't turn up," I reminded her—there was the time when the woman wouldn't let me in the office and she turned off the lights and locked the door, and the other time when we had an appointment at Montesquieu and she just didn't show up.

She asked me the date and said, "Oh, that was my day off."

Why make an appointment with a homeless woman on your day off? You think we need to walk around more?

Francois was right there. He'd been listening to the whole thing, and he stood up and said to Suzanne, "This is a big problem. It's a real problem. She can't stay on the street, you know. You have to do something, you have to get her off the street, and you have to help her."

And miraculously, when a French man said that, Suzanne didn't even have to make a phone call. She looked up, snapped her fingers, and said, "Oh yeah, I have a place you can stay."

She said there was a new shelter opening near place Monge, and she was going to be working there and could get me in after the first of the year. But before that, she would get me a bed at another shelter near Porte de Choisy.

She said it was too late to arrange for me to go there tonight, but I could come by in the morning and pick up the paperwork. And by the way, there was a tent in a back room over at Montesquieu that I could have for the night.

I was astonished. She had had that address all the time. She didn't even have to look it up or make a phone call. She had known a place I could sleep the whole time. All the nights I walked in the freezing weather trying to avoid the wolves, I could have been safe in a bed, in a shelter.

To be honest, I wasn't sure I believed her. All those weeks of disappearing and not showing up for appointments, she wouldn't help me until Francois, a French man, one of her own, stood up for me.

But that was all in the past now,.and I had to put it behind me, let it go. She appeared to be willing to help me now, and that was what I had to focus on.

Suzanne took me over to Montesquieu to pick up the tent from the back room. She emerged with a bag, and I started opening it up to see how it worked, but it was the end of the day and I guess she wanted to go home. She said, "Don't bother. Chex knows how to work it. You'll set it up beside hers, won't you?"

Then she took off.

So I went over to where Chex was set up—I knew she'd be in her tent pretty much all day, because it was so cold out—and I hollered, "I have a tent!"

Chex came out, took one look at it, and said, "Oh no. That's not good." See, Suzanne had tried to give her that tent too, and she said you just couldn't set the thing up; it was a disaster. She went right back in her tent and wouldn't touch the thing.

But I figured anything was better than walking all night. I really wanted to sleep in that tent. I couldn't walk another night. Chex wouldn't budge, but Katharine, who slept in a tent right beside her, came out to help. And Chex knew a guy from Poland, Jonas—he came over to help out too.

It took hours. The tent was missing a bunch of stuff, and we ended up with this little collapsed teepee. It didn't zip or anything, and there were gaps where the wind blew in, but when I crawled inside the tent, you couldn't see me, I was covered. I was sleeping alongside Chex and Katherine and I knew—I hoped—that if I screamed they would help me out.

It was fairly warm, and I slept until I had to go out to the magic toilet, but after that my body heat was all gone and I froze. It was too cold to sleep. Even so, it was way better than walking all night.

After that episode with the tent, Chex called me "American Catastrophe."

⚜ ⚜ ⚜

When Suzanne arrived at Agora the next morning, I was there waiting. She gave me some paperwork sealed in an envelope and said everything was OK for me to have a bed at a women's shelter. She showed me where it was, near Porte de Choisy—way over south of Paris.

I was carrying my big backpack as well as a plastic bag, and I didn't have any metro tickets, but she gave me one. Then I asked if she could map it for me on Google—she had a computer—but she just told me the name of the metro stop again and said, "Just ask." I reminded her I didn't speak much French, that sometimes it was hard to get directions from people. But she just said, "Look for the big church, the place you're looking for is right next door, on rue des Malmaison." Finally, Sabrina said she would Google Map it for me.

It was a five-minute walk from the Maison Blanche metro stop—that was pretty funny, going from a metro stop named White House to a street named Bad House, which is what Malmaison means. It's a weird name for a street with a women's homeless shelter on it, and it wasn't so very easy to find.

On the corner of the street beside the church was a wall of graffiti and an old brick building that wasn't in great shape. There was just a little side door open, with no sign outside, and indoors there was a flight of steps.

I went up and opened the door onto a small landing with an armchair on it. There was a room opposite with the door half ajar, and I could see a desk with some paperwork and files, but there was nobody inside. I went looking for someone along the corridor, but nobody seemed to be in, so I kept climbing the stairs. On the third floor I found a toilet and went in there. Everything was stained and looked a little dirty, but I'd seen worse.

I started knocking on doors, and at the fourth or so door, someone answered. It was Dani, a woman I had seen at the women's group at Montesquieu. She was small—like really small, maybe 4'10"—and she had light-brown hair cut short like a man's and almost always wore a red-and-black lumberjack coat. She didn't speak English, but she was kind.

She looked at my papers and said something in French that I didn't understand, and then motioned for me to follow her. We went back outside and walked around the corner to another old building, also pretty run down. Up a flight of stairs and through a couple of doors was what looked like a dining hall. There was someone in the kitchen and she talked to them and then motioned for me to follow her again. Up another flight of stairs to the right, two more doors, and we were at the office.

I think Natalie was the employee on duty that day. She was a beautiful French woman with naturally curly brown hair that fell to her shoulders, and she always dressed really nicely. I showed her the paperwork and she took me back to the first building to find a man named Victor.

Victor didn't speak English either, so we communicated with gestures. He went over to a locked closet and emerged with an armload of stuff. He showed me a toothbrush and toothpaste and soap, and put his palms up and shrugged his shoulders, miming, did I need any of this stuff? I said, "Way yes," and nodded like crazy.

Then he took me up to the third floor, to a room with three other beds, and gave me a coated sheet like the ones they used at Montesquieu. They're so small you can't tuck them in, so they never stay in place. If you turn over once, the thing will fall right off. But it was a sheet, and there was a bed and a clean room. I felt numb. I almost couldn't believe it. Victor turned the heat up in the room and showed me the toilet down the corridor that I used earlier, and the showers. There were three shower stalls with no lock on the doors, and they were a little grimy, but they did have curtains.

Victor was always very kind and respectful to all the women. He put his hand to his mouth and said "Mange" and pointed to the other building, and he showed me six o'clock on his watch, so I knew dinner was over there at six. When he left, I lay down on the bed he'd shown me to rest, and it felt so good to be in a warm room with no wolves.

Then it was dinnertime, and I got up and headed over to the dining room. There weren't many people there, so I figured maybe I was early, but there was lots of food. It was the same prepack-aged food you got at Agora—homeless food, in plastic containers—but it was hot and I was so thankful, just so thankful, to eat. I ate everything that was put in front of me, and it was a lot. Then I had a shower and went to bed. I was just so exhausted.

⚜ ⚜ ⚜

There seemed to be a TV room nearby, so I lay awake and listened to the noise of the show and the women laughing and talking as they sat around watching it. They kept going till at least midnight, and I wondered what time they'd be waking us up in the morning. Would it be six or six thirty, like at Montesquieu?

I drifted off to sleep, but I was constantly awakened by the pain in my feet. It was a constant throbbing that wouldn't stop, followed by waves of sharp knife-stabbing pain. I pulled out my backpack and propped them up on that, and it felt so good to lie down and stretch out.

Nobody woke anybody up the next morning. I woke as the sun was rising, and I kept expecting someone to knock on the door and yell like at Montesquieu, but it was unbelievably quiet. The women in the room with me kept on sleeping. One of them was a small elderly woman, who breathed so lightly she almost didn't seem to be moving. Her eyes were strangely unwrinkled, and she looked peaceful.

At around seven I got out of bed, and went over to the dining hall to see what was going on. There was coffee and bread. I drank two big, sweet cups and ate some bread and butter with sugar, and when I got back to the room, all the others were still sound asleep, so I took my boots off and crawled back under the covers.

That afternoon one of the people who worked there came and motioned for me to pick up my stuff and leave the room. We walked down to the door and my heart sank. I thought it meant they were putting me back on the street. But he took me outside, then around the corner to the other building, to a room on the third floor with two beds. A beautiful Asian woman opened the door. He asked her if she spoke English, and she smiled and said, "A little."

Her name was Ji-Min, and she was a little taller than me, maybe 5'5". She had long, sleek, dark hair and a beautiful face and spirit. The room was really nice—it was a small room, but that's why there were only two beds in it. There was a little table and a chair, and Ji-Min had hung a little mirror above the sink, and she'd stuck papers with Korean words written on them in black magic marker that kind of danced across the wall. There were two small closets and the one on my side of the room had a padlock on it, but that was OK. I put my stuff under the bed.

I had a bag of tobacco from picking up cigarettes and some rolling papers I had bummed from someone at Agora, and I started to try to roll a cigarette. But I wasn't very good at all. In fact, I was pretty bad. Watching me, Ji-Min burst out laughing and I did too. She motioned for me to come and sit on her bed, and she rolled a few cigarettes for me as we laughed together, and I was so relieved that I hadn't been put back out on the street.

Then we went downstairs and smoked together. I was only in Ji-Min's room for two nights, but I believe we will be friends forever.

⚜ ⚜ ⚜

Ji-Min told me parts of her story. She explained that it was very complicated, and most people didn't understand it. She was married to a Frenchman in 2004, but her husband started doing drugs and he would throw her into the door repeatedly while he beat her. She even had to go to the hospital and get stitches a couple of times. She stayed with him for a while, and when he would start to beat her she would leave the apartment and walk all night. I bet it was really bad for her, because she was so pretty and looked so vulnerable.

Ji-Min always made me laugh. She told me one cold night she was walking, wearing only sandals on her feet and no coat, and she passed a dog with a warm coat on. She said that thinking back on it, she had to laugh: Sometimes dogs appear to be treated better than humans.

Finally she left her husband, and then it was time to renew her residency card. She went to her appointment at the prefecture, and she brought everything the police told her to bring: a letter promising her a job for one year, a domiciliation letter, and her old residency card to renew, but it was a trap.

They told her she would have to go back to Korea because she had no reason to stay in France. But she didn't want to leave France, it had become her home, so now she was stuck.

I spent two nights in Ji-Min's room, and then Djamila, who worked at Malmaison, came around and told me to take my things again and follow her. When I found someone who spoke enough English to translate why, she explained that I was staying on an emergency basis, and while the normal residents were out visiting friends or family for the Christmas holiday, they were just shuttling me around to whatever bed was vacant that night. So it made sense.

The next bedroom was just down the hall, and it was the same size as Ji-Min's, but it didn't have the same warm feeling. The walls were bare. There was only one closet this time and it was really full, so I stashed my stuff as usual under the bed. I didn't have much. Most of the bedrooms at Malmaison seemed to be crammed full of stuff—suitcases, boxes, and shopping bags full of clothes. Some of them smelled of spices and really foreign scents.

I was still really exhausted, and I was spending a lot of the time in bed, just so happy that nobody woke me up and pushed me out of the doors onto the street. At Malmaison they never did that—you didn't have to leave if you didn't want to.

It snowed, and one afternoon I made an Emmaus snowman—a snow mouse. I used plastic spoons for the ears, a pointy nose, and a paper crown on its head, and I stuck a cigarette in its mouth. It was right by the smoking area, and many of the women at Malmaison smoked, including staff. Everyone laughed at it and took pictures.

I kept thinking about how Christmastime was supposed to be. I know you need to be in the present moment, and I was trying, but on many levels I was still resisting. I missed my mom, and I kept thinking about how just before she died, I drove back from college to see her. It was the weekend after Thanksgiving, and she was already doing her Christmas shopping by mail order.

She told me to pick out something I'd like and she'd get it for me. At the time I had a pet cat, and I picked out this sterling-silver ring with five cats on it. It wasn't her taste at all, and she said, "Well, it's different," so I figured I didn't have a chance to get the cat ring. She asked me to pick out something else and I did, but inside I kept going back to the cat ring; I really liked it.

Then she died on December 10, very suddenly. I never got to say good-bye to her, but a few days before Christmas, the silver cat ring arrived in the mail. Even though she didn't like it, she knew how much I did and she bought it for me. It was right there on my hand, and I looked at it and remembered her.

⚜ ⚜ ⚜

In America I almost always worked on Christmas Eve, and usually Christmas Day and New Year's Eve too. I knew that after the holiday season it was tougher to find work, because none of the regular nurse's aides would take vacation or call in sick; they all needed to make up for what they spent over the holidays.

So every winter I would take any shift and work as many hours as I could, because I knew January through March it would be difficult to get forty hours a week and I wouldn't be able to make the bills.

It was kind of cool working Christmas Eve, because you could pick and choose where you wanted to work. I probably would have gone to one of the group homes or an assisted-living place like Irvington Village, so I could work with people I knew. Or I would have worked at Chloe's group home for medically fragile children. That would have been a fun place to hang out and help the kids celebrate Christmas.

I kept thinking about how Chloe had wanted to get her old fiber-optic Christmas tree out this year. We'd talked about it before

I left to go to Spain. We were really going to decorate. We had all kinds of plans.

✤ ✤ ✤

One afternoon I walked into Agora and there was some time free on the computer, so I checked my mail. There was an email from the nursing agency. They said Chloe had been phoning, asking where the January rent and the money I owed her that she wired me by Western Union were.

I emailed back to the agency that I was sorry, and she was going to have to sell my stuff to try and make up the rent I owed. She should be able to get two months' rent for the Jeep, daybed, and DVD collection, maybe more. I also asked them to remind her that the situation was out of my control; I was stuck in a foreign country, and unless they wanted to help me, I had no resources to get back home. I never heard from the nursing agency again.

So that was it. Everything was gone: the Jeep, the daybed with the most comfortable mattress I'd ever slept on in my life, no more DVDs, clothes, or apartment in America. It was hard to think about Chloe selling my stuff and renting out my room to somebody else, but I knew she would have to. She owed rent every month just like I did, and money was just as tight for her as it was for me in America.

It meant that, for the moment anyway, my life back in America was gone. I remember walking through the Jardin des Halles and reflecting on something I recently read in *A New Earth*: "Sometimes letting go is an act of far greater power than defending or hanging on."

I had some two-day-old bread in my pockets, too hard to eat, and there was frost crunching under my boots. The air was clear and little frozen icicles hung off the plants. As soon as I sat down, a flock of pigeons started landing beside me, so I started feeding them. I used to do that all the time in America.

A park warden came up and told me not to; he said it was *interdit* forbidden, and showed me his little book of official tickets, like he would give me a fine for feeding the birds. But I fed them anyway, as soon as he left. So many of them had problems with their feet, like they'd been caught up in traps, and many of them had string tangled around at least one of their feet. They were such tiny little things. Some of them had already lost a foot, and many of the others were limping. Their feet were so much worse than mine.

One of them had a piece of string tangled around both feet, and it was so bad he couldn't move each foot independently. He wobbled when he walked like he was having trouble keeping his balance. He was going to lose one foot for sure. I remember thinking, *My pain is nothing compared to yours.* I had to help him.

If I could get the string off, maybe one foot would survive. He wouldn't let me get close enough to untangle it with my hands. He looked like he was starving, and he ate the bread crumbs faster than I could put them down. I bummed a cigarette and burned the string off with the lit end, being careful not to burn his skin, and it worked! I couldn't get all the string off because he kept trying to get away, but he couldn't move fast enough, and when I finished he could move his feet independently.

That reminded me of Lester, a horse I used to care for back in Louisiana, when I was twenty and worked as an assistant trainer in a racehorse stable, before I decided to go to college. When you work the racetrack in America, your biggest fear is the meat wagon. When a horse breaks its leg during a race or in a morning workout, the meat wagon picks it up and takes it to the parking lot behind the stables, where one of the vets comes with a huge syringe. Before the syringe is empty, the horse is trembling to the ground.

Lester was a tall, dark, bay thoroughbred racehorse with a dark mane and tail. He had big brown eyes and a huge heart, and he loved carrots. Lester was a 1,200-pound allowance-class stallion— allowance is one step down from a stakes race. The Kentucky Derby is a popular stakes race.

Usually stallions are very aggressive, but Lester possessed a most gentle spirit, and he looked exactly like the model horse I dreamed of and got for Christmas as child. Lester was owned by Dr. Joe K. Lester, his namesake.

One morning Lester was working out with his favorite jockey, Rickey Frazier, aboard when all of a sudden his head bobbled, and his moves became sharp and jagged. Rickey pulled him up fast and jumped to the ground. I looked up and the meat wagon was headed straight toward him.

Most racehorses only represent money to their owners and trainers. If the horse is a high-class stallion or mare, and it breaks a leg, sometimes the owner will invest the time and money to repair the leg and breed it. Lester was an allowance-class stallion, named after his owner, so I hoped.

We loaded him into the meat wagon and took him back to the barn. The vet came right away and x-rayed the leg. It was a very bad break. Lester would never race again, but the owner wanted to try to save him for breeding purposes.

Lester and I, well, we were the same, and we both knew it. I loved him the way a mother loves her child. Lester spent about two weeks in the hospital after his operation. Usually horses are sent to a calm, quiet farm to heal, but it was as if Dr. Lester knew we needed to be together for him to heal. He made the unusual choice to bring Lester back to the racetrack to recover for thirty days.

I knew this would probably be our last thirty days together, so I spoiled him every chance I got. He had this huge cast on his leg, from his hoof all the way up his leg, almost to his chest.

If he was in too much pain to get up, I would go into his stall, sit beside him, and give him the equivalent of a bed bath and comb his mane and tail. Sometimes I would stay half the night with him, often sleeping curled up next to him in his stall. I trusted him completely, as I knew he would never hurt me.

I also ordered a fifty-pound bag of carrots that stayed right outside his stall. People would come to visit from all over the racetrack: This was a truly unique situation. Lester was very clever: He learned quickly how to work the people. They would look at the big cast and say, "Oh, poor baby." Then Lester would take his broken leg and stretch it out in front of him. He would rub the cast with his nose for a moment. Then he would reach for the bag of carrots, stretching his neck out long while licking his lips. Almost everyone would relent and give him a carrot.

When the thirty days were up, it was time for Lester to go to his new home. Dr. Lester assured me I could call and check on him or make the long drive to visit him whenever I wanted, and I did. He seemed to adjust well to his new life.

But the following year, one of the vets who had operated on Lester came to see me in person. He explained that Lester had been dismounting a mare and put too much weight on his bad leg. It broke for a second time, and they were rushing Lester back to the hospital; I immediately dropped everything and rushed to the hospital to meet him.

They had decided not to operate again, and they were getting ready to put a fiberglass cast on his leg. When Lester saw me come in the hospital door, he started nickering. The vets smiled and said, "He is talking to you, he is very happy to see you."

They asked if I wanted to take the lead rope and stand by his head. Of course, I did. They explained what they were going to do, and that it would get very hot on Lester's leg. They said it wouldn't be too painful, but it would be uncomfortable, so I should be careful because sometimes horses bit when they were doing it.

But I trusted Lester completely. No matter how much pain he was in, I knew he loved me and would never hurt me. He rested his head on my shoulder. When it became painful, his neck would go limp, so I would carry most of the weight of his head on my shoulder, and I was happy to do so. I caressed his face and petted his neck, and a few times he raised his lips, showing his teeth as he ground them, then he would put his head back with his teeth resting on top of my shoulder, being very careful not to harm me.

It was much harder for the leg to heal the second time. In fact, the vets believe it never completely healed. It didn't fuse together the way they hoped it would.

The next breeding season, his leg gave way again. As much as Lester loved life, it was decided that the most humane thing to do would be to get that big syringe out, which he had so narrowly escaped twice before.

I took comfort knowing he would feel no more pain in this lifetime, and that he had some offspring to carry forward that big, warm heart and kind, gentle spirit.

I looked back down at the pigeons, and what I'd left behind me in America didn't seem that significant anymore. I was here in Paris, so this was where I was meant to be at this moment of my life.

And if I didn't want to be in a shelter or walking on the street, I would just have to get it together. I never had much trouble finding work, so maybe I could find a job and an apartment and make a go of it here.

It was a very cold Christmas Eve, and I wanted to be with someone who cared, so I walked over to where Chex had her tent, on the other side of the Jardin des Halles.

Chex was glad to see me, so we went over to the soup line at Saint-Eustache to have dinner together. They always had the best soup, and they were very kind. After we ate, everyone started lining up again, so Chex and I got back in line too, and they gave us a present!

It was a big one, wrapped, with a ribbon, and I was overwhelmed—giving Christmas gifts to homeless people. When I opened it up, it was a beautiful pink polar-fleece blanket, and it was the softest, warmest blanket I've ever owned.

I understand that we shouldn't identify with material possessions or get attached to them, but I cherish that blanket. It reminds me how special the community at La Soupe Saint-Eustache is; it truly is one of the most spiritual places I have ever been.

⚜ ⚜ ⚜

It was way after dark when I walked back to Porte de Choisy from Saint-Eustache, and it was a really long walk, so I draped the blanket around my shoulders to keep me warm. I went down to the river and crossed over by place du Châtelet to Saint-Michel. Then I walked along the water, and I took a moment to appreciate the beautiful form of Notre Dame. I crossed over Boulevard Saint-Germain to rue Monge, and all the way down avenue des Gobelins—that always gave me a laugh, gobelins—to place d'Italie, and then there was just avenue de Choisy to go.

It's a cool neighborhood, and there didn't seem to be as many wolves as there were around the heart of the city. There'd be lights on in all the Asian restaurants and all the grocery stores would still be open, all lit up, with the strangest-looking kinds of Asian fruit for sale outside. It reminded me a little bit of New Orleans; it felt a little funky, but fairly safe.

11

Different Perceptions

When I got back to Malmaison, I went upstairs with the blanket. I knew they had a Christmas party going on in the dining hall, and I didn't feel like taking part in the whole thing, but someone saw me come in and they came and got me.

There weren't a lot of people. Many of the residents had left to be with family or friends, but they had sandwiches and rich desserts, bowls of peanuts on the table, bottles of Coca-Cola, and music on the radio.

Everyone wanted me to be having fun, they were friendly and everything, but I just wasn't into it. I was tired, and in a lot of pain from all the walking. It takes two hours for me to walk each way, to and from Châtelet.

I finally made it back upstairs. The bedroom window looked out right onto the large church next door, and it being Christmas Eve, there was a service with beautiful music. It sounded like a large choir. I thought about going over there, but couldn't force my feet back into the boots, so I enjoyed it from my bed. I listened to them laughing outside and singing all night; they didn't stop till dawn.

This was all new to me. In the United States, we have midnight mass, but it's over by one or two in the morning, and then everyone goes home.

On Christmas I stayed in bed most of the day. I was tired, and my feet and stomach ached. I had my cycle, and this may be more information than you need to know, but actually that stuff is really annoying when you're homeless. I used to meditate, and tell my body, "Stop cycling," because where do you go for tampons if you don't have any money? At Malmaison they had maxi pads, but they were enormous. They made me feel really strange, like I had a big long tail, way up my back, and of course they didn't have any medicine for cramps, so on Christmas Day I took it easy, and did some stretching and meditating.

⚜ ⚜ ⚜

The day after Christmas my roommate came back from wherever she was visiting over the holidays. She was from Morocco and she looked to be in her twenties. I asked her if she spoke any English and she didn't, but she seemed nice. After a short while, a woman called Hind, who was also from Morocco, came by, and she did speak English. She was a thin woman, about twenty-eight, I'd guess, wearing sweatpants, with long, dark, wavy hair and glasses. She asked me where I was from and I told her America.

She seemed surprised, and sniffed and threw her nose into the air and said, "I thought maybe England," and I knew I was being judged once again because of where I was born.

Hind told me she had been at Malmaison for years, because her situation was so special, and she waited for a moment, like she was expecting me to ask about her very special situation. I didn't want to feed into her drama, so I remained silent, and then she asked how I got into Malmaison.

I said something about how a French gentleman helped me with the social worker. I didn't realize that later, influenced by that special Arabic stereotype, she'd be telling people how American women will have sex with just about anybody they see, and how I was supposedly sleeping with all these different men she made up.

But Hind was like that. She was a real troublemaker, and she had a real haughty manner. She was always gossiping about the other women too, not just me, and acting like she ran the place, always telling people what to do.

I asked one of the social workers about her behavior, and she said, "For someone like Hind, who's been here so long, that's all she has, the power to mess with people." Still, I can't understand how a person can get pleasure from hurting other people like that. I couldn't help but think if she took all that energy and turned it around into positive action, she could have been out of there a long time ago.

As the regular residents began trickling back into Malmaison from their family visits or wherever they'd gone, I could already feel the different kinds of tension starting to shape up. But I stayed out of it, and I guess I was getting used to the idea that I was safe, for a little while anyway. I knew I was only going to be at this shelter for a short time, but I wasn't headed back out on the street right away, or at least it didn't look like it, and I could kind of relax.

I started to hang out with some of the other women, and we smoked cigarettes together and drank tea in their bedrooms. Ji-Min was the best, but I also liked South America: She was the amazingly kind elderly Brazilian lady whose room I slept in the first night.

When I first met her and she found out I was from America, she said, "You're North America and I'm South America!" and laughed. She would always greet me, "Hey, North America!" and I would reply "Hey, South America!" It was an ongoing joke between us, a lot of fun, and her eyes were bright blue and kind of radiated peace.

She told me she was from a rich state in southern Brazil and she moved to Europe with her husband, who set up a business doing importing. But he died suddenly of cancer, and when she'd spent the money he left her, she began selling things until she had nothing left to sell.

She was very small and neat, and unlike many of the residents, she had very little stuff and was always happy and even-tempered.

Another woman I got to know was from Pakistan, and that's what I always called her. I never was good with names; they're just labels anyway, they can't truly describe who we are. She introduced herself to me one day and encouraged me to keep trying to learn French. She said it was a very difficult language and she had found it really hard to learn, but I shouldn't give up, I must practice courage.

Pakistan told me that she'd been living at Malmaison for two years, and she had trouble getting divorced. She said at first her husband was refusing to sign the papers, but he eventually did, and the social workers gave her a grant to go to a great school to learn French. She had wanted to quit many times, but she hung in there, and now, after a long period of unemployment, she had a part-time job. It was at Monoprix, a chain store kind of like a Fred Meyer in America, but more expensive.

And there was Liza. She was from somewhere in Africa and there was a war going on where she had lived. She had two grown children that lived in France, and she moved here several years ago when she was diagnosed with a heart condition. She had her own restaurant back home, but now she just worked at a local bistro. She was always trying to give me shoes, but with my bad feet they never fit comfortably. Liza was always kind and thoughtful. She didn't speak any English, but we managed to communicate.

Aicha had a job too, and I really liked her. She was Algerian, about twenty-eight, and spoke a little English. She had a French–English dictionary, so we'd look words up in that. She always wore a dark-blue stocking cap, never put on any makeup, always swaddled herself up in large sweaters, and hid her hair under the hat. But when you saw her without her hat, she had beautiful long dark hair, and she instantly went from looking like a tomboy to a beautiful woman.

I know we're not supposed to be preoccupied with physical form, that our bodies are merely shells that we temporarily inhabit, but the physical transformation was amazing. I didn't need to know Aicha's story or exactly what had happened so that she ended up living in a homeless shelter. It was obvious she'd been through a lot, and she'd decided to hide herself from the wolves. It was her survival tactic. Maybe if I'd been on the street longer, I would have taken that route too.

Like almost all the women from Arabic countries who lived at Malmaison, Aicha wore Western clothes. There was only one woman who wore the Muslim headscarf, and she was one of the quietest and kindest there. Most of the residents were African, and a lot of them wore long elaborate robes and turbans. When you saw two or three of them together, they looked like ships, sailing grandly down the street.

Almost all the women at Malmaison had cell phones, and they all seemed to have at least some money, even the ones that didn't have a job, which was a lot of them. They'd buy food on the street and take it to their rooms, and they'd have packs of cigarettes, maybe a new blouse from time to time.

I started asking where they got the money from, and one of them, Caroline, a nice-looking African woman with dark-red hair extensions, said that Pierre, one of the social workers, had gotten her a grant. She said she had an appointment with him one morning and by that afternoon she had cash in her hand to buy some personal items she needed and a phone; in France you can't find a job without a phone.

She also said when she first came to town a few years ago she didn't have any money or metro tickets, so she went to the American Church and asked for help. Even though she wasn't American, they helped her because English was her second language. She said they gave her money and metro tickets, and I should go see them to ask for help.

So I went to the American Church after that and asked for help with metro tickets, money for tampons, and a phone. They said they didn't help people anymore, and they suggested I go to the American embassy.

I explained I had already gone to the embassy and they had told me I needed to go to the French embassy, and I didn't I have the finances to do that. They just repeated the same answer, that they didn't help people anymore.

So I went to see Pierre. He was always nice. He had a good smile and a little Buddha belly that made him look wise and gentle. I asked him if he could give me some metro tickets or a cash grant.

But he said he couldn't help me because I was only at Malmaison temporarily, so he couldn't use the funds for me. That seemed logical, but he said I should talk to the social workers at the next place I was headed to, and they would work it out for me there.

⚜ ⚜ ⚜

They started a new French class at Agora three times a week, Monday, Wednesday, and Friday. I walked two hours each way, but every time, the teacher never showed up, so then I would walk back to Mal-maison.

Sometimes I would hang around and watch the people ice-skating at the skating rink they set up outside the city hall. It felt funny being around tourists, especially Americans. In a way it was more comfort-able, because I could understand what they were saying, but it made me think that not so long ago, I was a tourist just like them.

People would ask me where Notre Dame was and I could tell them, but it made me wish I was still one of them, because they could just go home.

One time I was walking by a park close to Notre Dame on my way into Châtelet. I guess it was Sunday, because there were lot of people dressed up, and I felt out of place. I was cold and I sat down in the park and thought, *What am I doing I don't belong here.*

I looked down at my clothes. I was wearing sweatpants and a jacket with a ripped hood, and my boots were basically falling apart, and I thought, *These don't belong here.*

I sat on the park bench shivering for a few moments, then I got up, and there was a black faux-fur coat just lying on the fence of the little fountain that was in the middle of the park. Someone folded it up and just laid it there. It looked so warm. So I sat back down and looked at it for maybe half an hour. I kept thinking someone would come back for it, but no one did, so I picked it up, and it fit. There were a few bald spots, but it was really warm.

It felt like a sign. My mom loved fur coats, even in Louisiana. She loved the mink my father bought her when I was a child. In Paris the park is the thrift store. When people get tired of something, instead of throwing it out, they leave it in the park for someone less fortunate to pick up, so now I had a faux-fur coat to keep me warm, and it was really cold. When I looked back on this later, I realized I was identifying with my clothes, at that moment in my life.

⚜ ⚜ ⚜

Almost every day, Aicha asked if I had money or a metro pass, and every day I told her, "No, nothing." At first I felt frustrated that she asked the same question over and over, and then I began to understand it was her way of asking me if I wanted her to sneak me onto the metro with her. Sometimes she'd tell me what time she'd be leaving, so we could walk there together, and she'd sidle me through the turnstile with her, using her metro pass.

Aicha had a job on the Champs-Élysées at Quick, which was a burger joint in Paris similar to Wendy's in America, and Aicha loved to walk up and down the avenue window-shopping. It is a great place to pick up cigs, but she hated me doing that; she thought it was disgusting. Even though she didn't smoke, she would bum cigarettes from people and give them to me, so I didn't have to do it. I didn't mind that she felt that way. When I lived in Portland, cigarette smoke drove me nuts, so if I'd seen someone smoking cigs off the ground, I probably would have felt the same way.

But I thought she was just making herself depressed, the way she would window-shop so much, always longing for this really expensive stuff and then becoming miserable because she couldn't afford it. I tried to explain she didn't need all that stuff, but she didn't get it.

⚜ ⚜ ⚜

The whole time I was being shuffled around to different rooms, and just before New Year's they moved me again. They kept apologizing about it, but they said I'd been sleeping in someone's bed and she was due back. This time they brought me to a room with a no-entry sign on the door. It had a paint-pot and the word CONDAMNÉ written on it, so I figured the room was condemned, but it wasn't that bad. The paint was peeling and there were a few stains around, but it was OK, and my new roommate was great: a cute little gray mouse.

The mouse kept me up all that first night, gnawing through the wall to get inside the room. It made its way through early in the morning and I heard its little feet pattering on the floor as it ran across the room and started looking through a plastic bag that I'd stashed under the bed.

So the next night I put a little piece of peach tart that I'd saved from dinner on the floor, beside the hole that the mouse had gnawed in the woodwork. The mouse was quiet all night, and I wondered whether somebody had killed it, but when I got up and looked at the mouse hole, the peach tart was gone.

So the mouse and I developed an arrangement: I would leave a little food out for it, and it would be quiet and let me sleep.

"Today, more than ever before, life must be characterized by a sense of universal responsibility, not only nation to nation and human to human, but also human to other forms of life." —Dalai Lama

Then the heating system blew out. Like I said, the buildings at Malmaison weren't in terrific shape. The snow started falling thick and fast, so they hooked a space heater up in the dining hall, but there was nothing in the bedrooms or the bathrooms, and it was bitter cold. Along with a lot of the women, my roommate left again, to stay with family or friends.

I stood at the window of the empty bedroom looking at the snow, thinking what it would feel like to be walking and skidding all night on that and what it would be like if I didn't have a bed.

It had been snowing a lot, and I knew there were a lot of other homeless people out there. The social services opened up a couple of metro tunnels to give them somewhere to sleep, but I knew it wouldn't be safe for women down there. There'd be nobody watching out for them after midnight. I was pretty sure that Chex would manage to get some shelter at Montesquieu, but I wondered about all the other women I'd seen.

I was still eating way beyond fullness, and packing my pockets with bread. Partly this was because I could almost never get back for lunch; once I'd walked to Châtelet, there wasn't time for me to walk all the way back again. But it was also as if I just couldn't throw it out, couldn't bring myself to do that. I knew there were people out there literally starving, and now I knew what it felt like to go days without food.

I'd been saving extra food in the fridge. You were allowed to do that so long as you labeled the bag, but after a while I knew I'd saved so much food I just couldn't eat it all. So every two or three days, I would take what I didn't need to the man who was always standing by the subway, begging for change. Or if he wasn't there, I would walk it over to place d'Italie and give it to the homeless people that lived in the metro tunnels.

The guy at metro Maison Blanche was always so appreciative. One day I only had some broccoli to give him because I'd run into a woman who looked really hungry and was very thin, and I gave some of the food to her. Then I thought, *Oh no, he's a guy, he's not going to go for the broccoli,* but he was still so grateful. So any time I could, I'd look for him.

One day a couple of the women asked me what I did with the food, and after that some of them started giving me extras if there was too much for them to eat, like a yogurt or something they didn't want.

⚜ ⚜ ⚜

There was another party at the shelter on New Year's Eve. There weren't any men because they didn't let men into Malmaison, except the ones who worked there, so it was just women, dancing together and talking. They had the radio on playing American pop and then some of the African women began putting CDs of music I guess maybe from Congo, or somewhere in Africa, and it was fascinating to watch them dance.

But my heart wasn't really into any kind of party. I knew I had to go to the new shelter on place Monge in a couple of days, and I hoped everyone would be as kind there as they had been at Malmaison.

But when I woke up the morning I was supposed to go to place Monge, there were several inches of new snow on the ground and it was still snowing really hard. I knew I was going to have to walk to place Monge in the snow because I still had no metro ticket, and it was a long hike. So I went to the office again, to ask one last time for a metro ticket, and they said sorry, they couldn't do that, but they also said I couldn't go out in this weather. They said I should stay another night and they would call the other shelter and warn them that I'd be coming a day late.

The next morning there wasn't much snow falling, but there was a lot on the ground, and it was very icy in places. But I made my way to place Monge, which was about two and half miles, or four kilometers. About one third of the way there, I stopped at the mall on place d'Italie and went inside to warm up. It was freezing and there was ice and snow everywhere. I even went inside a magic toilet about another half mile, or one kilometer, down the road to warm my hands.

The shelter was on a street that sounded like Vulcan—rue Vauquelin. Suzanne was there, and they had me sit in a room and brought me coffee while I waited for her to show me around.

It was a beautiful old six-story building, with a lot of stairs, and I was on the top floor. Suzanne told me if I had come there a day earlier, I could have had a better room, but they were all taken now. I asked, "Didn't they call you from Malmaison and tell you I'd be a day late?" She said, "No, I didn't receive any phone call." Like I said, her English was way better all of a sudden. We climbed up to the top floor and walked through a room with three beds to a smaller room behind it with two beds. These two bedrooms shared their own little bathroom, with a shower and a toilet (with an actual toilet seat—what a nice surprise).

At Malmaison everyone shared the same toilets and showers; there were only two or three shower stalls per floor, and they were open only at certain times. I remember thinking, *Wow, I can take a shower any time I want,* and as for the toilet seat, I was getting used to not having one. It wasn't a big deal anymore, I was adapting, but I must admit it was much more comfortable, and I really appreciated it.

Suzanne said I could stay three or four weeks at rue Vulcan, and for the whole time I'd be in the smaller room with two beds. She didn't explain what would happen after my month was up, but I thought it might be enough time for me to get back on my feet and get a job, maybe find a little room to rent.

My new roommate was American too. She was African American, and maybe about fifty; she wore glasses and a stocking cap, and when I first set eyes on her, I honestly thought she was a man. She had a big belly but no hips like a man, and her body and face were so masculine looking, I thought perhaps this place was like Montesquieu, where there wasn't enough room and the men and women had to sleep in the same room together. But the room on the second floor at Montesquieu was huge, and this room was small, and it was just the two of us, so I was pretty concerned about that.

I did realize she was a woman after we spoke, and she said her name was Sky. She said she'd been in France for two and a half years, and she loved the street, loved being homeless. I couldn't understand that. Being homeless is brutal, how could anyone like it? But I realized pretty quickly that Sky wasn't stable at all.

She said she'd been in a hospital where they put drugs in her food to make her sleep, and with my nursing experience, that made me wonder if she might be violent. In the United States we wouldn't hide drugs in somebody's food, but if someone was violent toward staff or other patients, we'd ask a doctor to prescribe a tranquilizer, so I was very careful with her.

The first night was very noisy. I didn't get much sleep, but it was OK because women were coming in off the street all night, and I was glad they had a place to stay.

At six thirty in the morning, a woman came and turned the lights on, and clapped her hands and said, "Everyone up!" We had to leave the building by eight and we couldn't come back till after five. I guess I'd been spoiled at Malmaison. Sure, it was an older building in need of some refurbishment: There was no heat most of the time, the toilets didn't have seats, and one of them, along with the showers, was locked for a large portion of the day and all night. But those are material things, and when it came to being off the street, out of the weather, and away from the wolves, Malmaison was the Ritz.

At Malmaison you could stay in bed all day if it was really cold out or you were hurting, but here you got up and had a quick "breakfast" of café, bread, and jam. Then you put some in your pocket for lunch, and you were out the door with your stuff, just like Montesquieu.

After breakfast I saw everyone getting all their stuff together and the workers asked me, "Are you coming back tonight?" and I thought, *Oh no*. I explained what Suzanne had said, that it was all worked out for me to stay three or four weeks, but the guy at the door laughed and said this place on Vulcan was on a night-by-night basis. He said, "If you think you're coming back tonight, we can save your bed for tonight, but for weeks, no, we can't do that."

I would have to leave the building every day with my stuff, and every day I had to tell them my name and say that I would be coming back that night, or they wouldn't save my bed.

I felt so disillusioned. I hunted down Suzanne and explained what they'd told me, and she said it was a new place, they were working on it. Like they didn't have clothes hangers and she had no metro tickets to give out, and when I asked about a grant for a phone to get a job, she just laughed. "It's a new place, we don't have any resources."

⚜ ⚜ ⚜

So I walked into Agora every morning and spent most of the day there, but it was very cold outside, so the place was really crowded, and I was lucky to find a chair to sit on. I was really limping by this time, but I managed to find a chair near the paperwork guy from Pakistan.

We talked about how he wasn't staying at Montesquieu anymore because of all the bugs. They never washed any-thing, and he joked that the underground parking garages were cleaner. I started rubbing my boots, and he said, "Yeah, I know, it's the same for all of us. The street is horrible for your feet, you need to see the doctor, maybe she could give you some ointment to help out."

I said it wasn't that bad, I wasn't really sick, but he said he would translate for me if the doctor didn't speak English, so he took me back to the office where there was always a line of people waiting.

Dr. Schwartz did speak English, and she was a mature woman with short gray hair, a little stern looking but very kind. She looked at my feet and said, "This is bad." She kept saying, "There's nothing I can do," and I could tell she was frustrated about it. She had to do something, so before I put my boots back on, she made a Band-Aid with gauze and tape and put it on the biggest lump on the sole of my left foot.

She also gave me some paracetamol and a couple of Ultram, which is a pill they give you for chronic pain. Then she asked me if I had a French social security card and I said no, not yet, she said that was too bad, because I needed to see a specialist.

Then she spent half an hour on the phone trying to get ahold of someone who would see me without health insurance, and finally she managed to make an appointment for me at Saint-Vincent de Paul Hospital.

The nice Pakistani man who encouraged me to see her was waiting for me when I came out of her office. The Band-Aid was actually putting more pressure on the tumor and making it hurt worse, so I took off my boot to remove it. He smiled and said, "They put a Band-Aid on your tumor? That should make it go away."

We both cracked up laughing, then I explained to him she felt helpless, she wanted to do something, and that was all she could do. Because at that moment I hadn't realized just how much Dr. Schwartz had really helped me. See, Dr. Schwartz asked me where I was staying, where I slept, whether I could rest up during the day. And I explained I used to be in a good shelter where you could stay all day, but now I was in a new one where I had to leave at eight in the morning.

She shook her head and said, "This is no good. You shouldn't be walking all day on those feet." She wrote a letter requesting that I be moved to a shelter where I had the option of staying inside, so if I was having a painful day, I could prop my feet up. And her letter also stated that I shouldn't walk long distances, and requested that I receive a metro pass.

Dr. Schwartz told me I should give the letter to the social workers at rue Vulcan, but by this time I'd learned that if you wait for a social worker to do something, especially paperwork, it might not ever happen. So I knew what I had to do: walk from Châtelet to the Malmaison shelter and show the letter to the social workers there.

So, I walked five or five and half miles (eight or nine kilometers) to Port de Choisy. It took a while—like I said, I had to walk slowly and pace myself—I guess probably two hours.

Delphine, the young social worker on duty, made a photocopy, and said she'd talk to the director of the center, because she thought a bed might open up in a week or so.

It was time to walk back to place Monge again, but it was worth it. The evening of January 8, I was told the good news: They had a bed for me at Malmaison. I could go there the next morning.

12

Olivia

It was about nine thirty in the morning when I walked back into the dining hall at Malmaison with my stuff. There was a beautiful blond woman with a camera there, and when I came in she took one look at me and said, "You're the American woman I've been hearing about."

I thought she was American at first, because she spoke great English with no accent, but she explained she was French and used to live in New York, and we started talking.

Olivia Gay was a photographer. She said she'd been hired to illustrate a book about African women in Paris, and she was taking pictures of women at the shelter. She wanted to take photos of every woman there and make copies for people if they wanted them, and she said, "I'd like to take your photo too."

I was exhausted and in pain, and I explained I would rather not; I never was comfortable in front of a camera, and I didn't see the point, since I wasn't African. Olivia said, "OK, maybe later," and she helped me walk my bags up to my new room. She even went and asked the social workers for a pillow, though they didn't give her one. I elevated my feet up and rested through lunch—hungry as I was, I couldn't make myself lace up my boots again to go down and get it.

But after lunch, Olivia came upstairs looking for me. So to humor her, I got up, put my boots on, and tried to look a little nicer. I went downstairs and she took some photographs. She gave me her phone number and said to call her if I needed help, like to translate something.

It just felt good to be back. Ji-Min was so happy to see me, and I guessed she must have worked on Delphine on my behalf, and maybe that's why I got the room. Delphine had written down on a paper that I could stay at Malmaison for thirty to ninety days.

It was comforting to be back at Malmaison. It helped me start to feel settled in France. There was still no heat, but i could relax a little knowing I had a safe place to sleep. It may not have been warm, but I had shelter and food, and I was safe from wolves.

⚜ ⚜ ⚜

I kept reading Eckhart Tolle, trying to work on awareness and acceptance. When I wasn't able to accept things, which was still a large part of the time, at least I was becoming more aware of when I was resisting. I remembered what he says:

> *If you find your here and now intolerable and it makes you unhappy, you have three options:*
>
> *- Remove yourself from the situation,*
>
> *- Change it,*
>
> *- Or accept it totally.*

Now, I couldn't just remove myself from the situation, because I had nowhere to go, no way to get home. In the long term, I could try to change the situation by looking for work, getting myself a job, getting back on my feet, and getting out of the shelter, but short term, I had to accept things.

⚜ ⚜ ⚜

My new roommate was great. Alice was from Cameroon and she had a good heart. We couldn't sit down and carry on a complete conversation, but we could make out some words, and mime some things out. She was very kind, and I was always happy to see her smiling face.

Alice was popular with everyone. She always had beautiful clothes, which she cleaned and pressed, and the room smelled of camphor and spices. Someone translated for her one day and she told me that she came to France from Cameroon a couple of years ago and became very sick. When she got out of hospital after six months, she had nowhere to go except the street, but I already knew at least some of that stuff because we'd already worked through it a bit:

"*Malade.* Hopital." (She had been sick, went to the hospital.)
"*Bloqué ici.*" (I got stuck here.)
We got the main things across. We were friendly.

⚜ ⚜ ⚜

Ninety percent of the women had at least a little bit of money and I didn't have one cent. Aicha kept insisting that I should go to Delphine or Pierre, and that they could work it out for me and give me money and a metro pass. So I went and asked again, but Pierre was out sick, and Delphine said they never gave out money, it never happened.

I made appointments with her, I asked her repeatedly for a metro pass. She kept reassuring me that I'd get one in February, but she said it was too late for a January pass, and I would just have to manage. She said, "It's too hard for me to get one for you. You're American, and that just makes it too hard."

The system was crazy. So many women around me had metro passes and meal tickets and restaurant vouchers and cash grants. One woman from Algeria even told me her social worker paid for her to go to England because she said she had contacts to look for a job there. She went there twice, and her hotel, everything was paid for, so she went shopping and saw friends, and I can't afford to buy a box of tampons?

No metro tickets, no job search—isn't that what a shelter is supposed to do, help you get back on your feet? It didn't make sense. It was like they'd already given up on me.

I thought maybe it was just Delphine. Some of the women gave me the names of their social workers. A lot of them had been in the system for years, so some of these social workers were way across town. I hunted them down for several days, mostly on foot, and they all said the same thing: You're American, we don't help Americans, you have to do it on your own, you're American, that means you want to be here, so you have to figure it out.

⚜ ⚜ ⚜

Some of the women were just plain comfortable at Malmaison: It seemed like they didn't really want to get out of there. Hind was real comfortable. I'd say Malmaison was her place. She was always talking about people, gossiping, spreading rumors, and generally bossing the whole place about.

I tried to stay away from Hind, and I couldn't understand how someone could be so comfortable in a place like that. She seemed to have no desire to leave, and I didn't get it, wanting to stay in a shelter for the rest of your time. I would imagine there would have to be a way out.

But even though a lot of the women were really nice, there could be a real undercurrent of craziness and hostility at Malmaison. A lot of the women were angry, not necessarily mad at me, just angry and hostile in general. It was a complex atmosphere, especially when Hind was heading up some kind of vendetta. People would just lash out over the smallest thing, like if your food had leaked on theirs in the fridge.

I guess some of these women had started to lose it a little bit; some of them weren't real stable, which is something I can understand, having lived in the street. Some of them were totally sane, they were just stuck there—wars were going on in the countries they were from: Pakistan, Afghanistan, and many parts of Africa. But there were other women that appeared fine on the surface, but once I talked to them and got to know them, I realized they really were not OK.

One night I couldn't sleep, so I went downstairs to smoke a cigarette. It was about eleven. There were a few women in the dining hall eating and talking. Because some of the women who lived there had jobs, they would get back late. All the staff didn't do this, but if Djamila was working, she would always save food for them and heat it up when they got back.

We started talking and I showed Aicha the SIM card I'd bought long ago, but it didn't work in my Google phone because it was locked. I asked her if she knew anyone who had a phone I could borrow. She said no, but Djamila broke in trying to tell me something in French, and one of the women translated: Djamila had an old phone I could use, and she'd bring it tomorrow.

You can't find a job without a phone number for people to reach you. Djamila just worked in the shelter, she wasn't any kind of social worker, but I felt like she helped me way more than the social workers did. What a big heart that woman had. I gave her a big, big hug.

✤ ✤ ✤

After about ten days, Olivia came back to give out these nice matte color photographs. I had another doctor's appointment—I was seeing Dr. Schwartz every week to pick up paracetamol—so I was just rushing out. Olivia said, "We really need to talk, because I'd really like to get someone to do an article about you and your situation."

I said, "Why? This place is full of homeless women, and they all have stories, and most of them have been homeless way longer than me."

But Olivia said, "I've been to a lot of homeless shelters and you're the only American woman I've ever seen." She said maybe an article would help me get a metro pass or maybe even find a job or a place to stay. I said I would think about it, and she said she would make some phone calls. She had the phone number at the shelter, but she gave me her cell number again and told me to call her in a few days.

✤ ✤ ✤

One evening, walking down to place d'Italie, I met Francois. In fact, we literally ran into each other on the street. I hadn't seen him since the day he saved me at Agora, the day he told Suzanne she had to do something to help me, and she did.

He gave me a hug and a little kiss on each cheek, which is a typical French greeting, and we spent a while catching up. He said he'd found a job in a garage, he was a mechanic, but he was still sleeping at Montesquieu. I told him how good it was to be at Malmaison and thanked him a bunch of times, and we exchanged phone numbers and agreed to see each other again soon.

⚜ ⚜ ⚜

Most people told me I'd never find work in France. They said many French people couldn't find work, and I couldn't even speak much French, so how could I possibly do it, but Aicha said they were wrong. She said if I tried hard enough, I would find something, and she gave me the address of the place where she'd found her job at Quick Burger. It was a center run by Emmaus. The metro stop was Porte de Saint-Ouen, which is way up north of Paris, almost at the end of line 13. It's not too hard to get to if you're on the metro, but it's really hard to walk there if you're in the south of the city, like we were at Porte de Choisy.

But according to Aicha, at this place you could use the Internet for pretty much as long as you wanted and they let you use the phone for free too. At Malmaison we could use the phones as long as it was a 01 call to Paris. But walking through town, I'd come across a free magazine in English called FUSAC, which had pages of job offers, but most of them came with cell phone numbers or numbers out of town.

So I walked to Saint-Ouen from Porte de Choisy. It's a very long haul, about eleven or twelve miles (eighteen or twenty kilometers), but I didn't take the most direct route. I was following street signs, and it's hard to explain, but French street signs have arrows and it's like they point differently. If there's a sign pointing right, there are usually several roads, and it isn't always easy to tell which right-hand road they mean.

Aicha told me I needed to speak with one of the women at the Center, Renée, but when I found her, she said she had other meetings and I would have to come back the next day with an appointment. But she said until then I could use the Internet, so I went online and I started looking for a job.

First stop was the website of FUSAC. I figured there'd be one, and sure enough, it had ads for jobs and cheap apartments just like one of the free magazines in Portland, and most of them were in English. Online you could page through it and zoom in on anything that looked interesting, and there were several jobs I felt qualified to do, like looking after an elderly person or young children. I knew I was qualified to do that.

Most of the jobs specified that they required people who spoke fluent French, but I took down the phone numbers of a few that didn't. One ad was from a telemarketing company that said it was looking for native speakers from several different countries, including native English speakers, so I sent them an email. I stayed at the center as long as I could. When it closed for lunch, I ate some of the bread I'd stashed from breakfast. It wasn't really a meal, but I was used to that.

I spent almost the whole afternoon on the Internet, and by the time I'd walked all the way back to Malmaison, it was way after dark, there was no dinner left, and I was exhausted. I had walked a total of about six hours, and my body was in pain, but my spirit was good. I was doing something constructive and moving forward. I felt like it had been a really positive day.

The next day I walked to metro stop Porte de Saint-Ouen again, and it was brutal. I started putting cups of water in the freezer, so I could ice my feet at night to help with the pain and swelling.

It was worth it, because Renée, the woman who met with me, had a pretty gruff manner at first. But she spoke really good English, and that was a relief, and she was very positive.

She told me, "If you're willing to come back here and really work at finding a job, if you're sincerely dedicated, and it looks like you are because you stayed all day yesterday and here you are again today, then you will find work."

I was so glad to hear her say that. All these people were telling me no, you'll never be able to get a job. They were so negative. Everyone said this except Aicha, and here was this woman being so positive and supportive. That really stood out.

Renée wanted me to come in to the Emmaus Internet center every Monday. I explained about the metro situation, how I was walking to the north of Paris from Porte de Choisy, which is south of Paris, so I couldn't be there early in the morning. She said, "I can get your social worker to give you metro passes once or twice a week and a voucher for food. I'm not going to lock up here and go to lunch knowing you have nothing to eat. I will call Malmaison and fix it."

I watched her make the phone call, and Delphine told her if she put it in writing, she'd do her best to make it happen. That was a breath of fresh air.

Finally progress was being made. Like Jesus said,

> Ask and it will be given to you; seek and you will find; knock and the door will be opened to you. For everyone who asks receives; he who seeks finds; and to him who knocks, the door will be opened.

I felt like it was going to be OK; the door was beginning to open.

⚜ ⚜ ⚜

Delphine kept her word about the metro tickets and restaurant vouchers. She gave me twenty tickets to last till the end of January, and two restaurant vouchers worth three euros each. One metro ticket is only good for one ride, so if you have more than one appointment a day, it's easy to use up three or four. This was the middle of January, so I still had to walk a lot, but not everywhere, and certainly not from Porte de Choisy to Porte de Saint-Ouen.

And Delphine reminded me, this was just till February 1. That day I'd get a metro pass, and I could ride the subway for all of my appointments.

⚜ ⚜ ⚜

January 20 was the day President Obama was inaugurated, and the women at Malmaison had been talking about Obama nonstop. I remember I was walking into town that morning and I ran into an African woman I knew, and she said, "Where are you going to be this evening? You have to find a TV, right?"

I already had plans to go to Agora. I wanted to be with people from different cultures, and Francois said if he could get off work in time, he would watch the inauguration there. He called me once or twice a week since we literally ran into each other, and we tried to see each other every weekend, since he worked Monday through Friday. Sometimes we would just go for a walk in the park or down to the water and watch the dinner and tourist boats go by.

⚜ ⚜ ⚜

Agora was crowded, really packed. Paris is very diverse, and even more so in the homeless community. I guess everyone wanted to watch Obama and hear this black man speak, as he became president of America, the "strongest" country in the world. It was a pretty special feeling that evening, with all the homeless people at Agora. People from Africa, Pakistan, Korea, Eastern Europe, Arab countries—I never would have met all these people in America. Everyone wanted to come up and shake my hand because I was born in America. They all said, "Obama, good," and smiled.

Francois didn't make it, but Hakim, my self-appointed bodyguard from Montesquieu, came and stood next to me a good portion of the time, with his hand on my shoulder. And when Obama was sworn in, and they said his middle name, Hussein, it was great. All the Arabs, Afghans, Pakistanis, etc. stood up. They were clapping and cheering. It was beautiful.

Afterwards I pulled out my stash of cigar tobacco and handed it around and all these people from all over the world walked outside and smoked hand-rolled cigars together. Everyone was very nice and respectful. When people asked where I was from, I had begun telling them Earth, I am from planet Earth, because of the bad reaction I would get if they found out I was born in America. So, it had been a long time since it was OK to be born in America, but on that day it was. That day gave a lot of people hope.

As I walked back to Malmaison, I recalled how I was in Spain when Obama was elected, and during the campaign I was for Hillary Clinton. I remember talking to Donald, one of the nurses at Providence St. Vincent Medical Center, about the election. I said the most important things for me were ending the war and health care, and Hillary looked like she was going to really do something about those two things. But Donald was for Obama. He said, "Obama will bring people together. He's going to unite the whole world."

I didn't get it then, but seeing everyone from all those different countries cheering, coming together, it hit home. Donald was right: If only for a moment, it didn't matter what part of the planet anyone was born on; we were all the same, and it was kind of like Obama was the president of us all.

⚜ ⚜ ⚜

The next day I had my appointment at Saint-Vincent de Paul Hospital. The doctor was frustrated that I couldn't speak much French, but he could speak a little English. He said I needed surgery. He pointed at the growths on the soles of my feet and he said, "Those need to come out, that's disease, it's bad."

I guess he wrote something down saying I needed to get a French social security number, because the next time I saw Dr. Schwartz, she gave me the name of a social worker at Agora to go see. I ran into the paperwork guy, so he came with me in case I needed a translator. The social worker said I needed proof of when I arrived in France. After I had been in France for three months, I should come back with that proof and she'd try to help me get one. She was kind of gruff, and she huffed, "You haven't been here for three months, you can't get . . ." and then she opened my U.S. passport and she saw the beautiful eagle and went from being frustrated and stressed to suddenly being surprised and charmed—perhaps it brought her back to the present moment.

I told Dr. Schwartz I couldn't get surgery without a social security card, and she wrote a letter asking for me to get surgery even without health insurance. She said I should get Delphine to call them, so I wouldn't have to walk to Saint-Vincent de Paul just to make an appointment. She said Delphine should talk to the social worker at the hospital.

Delphine did call, but she told me they said if it wasn't an emergency, like it wasn't life-threatening, they wouldn't do it. I asked her, "Did you tell them how painful it is?" and Delphine just looked at me blankly and said, "Oh, is it painful?"

I kept going to Agora once a week to see Dr. Schwartz and pick up paracetamol and sometimes Ultram. She really rationed them out, and I only took them when I had to, so I could sleep, because the pain could be so bad it would keep me up all night long. One time I went in and she showed me the cupboard. She said, "I have nothing, not even any paracetamol." She said she relied on the government and they weren't giving her much of anything. She barely even had any gauze and tape left to make Band-Aids.

⚜ ⚜ ⚜

There were also French lessons. The class at Montesquieu just never worked out. The other students wouldn't show up and class would be canceled, or the teacher would have to leave early. I guess she had another job. So I started taking classes at a place called Halte Femmes near Gare de Lyon, but they had lot of mentally unstable women there in the main foyer. They would cancel class if it got too crazy, or if there was too much yelling, and that was almost every day.

And often the teacher would be pulled out of class to work the floor, or sometimes I would walk all the way over there and find that class was canceled for some other reason, like one time the room was being professionally cleaned. There were many days when it seemed like everyone in France was telling me how important it was that I learned French, but nobody wanted to teach me.

I was also going to Saint-Ouen every week to look for a job at the Emmaus office. One day Renée offered to let me use the phone. She said I could call anywhere, even America if I wanted to. But I guess I was already past that point by then. It felt like there was no one left in America I could call.

⚜ ⚜ ⚜

At the end of January, I went to the social workers' office to ask about getting a Navigo metro pass so I could ride the subway to get to appointments that were spread all over town. Delphine said she still hadn't received the money to buy the February passes, but she was sure it would come the next day. It had to—all of these other women were relying on their metro passes, not just me.

The next morning I went to the office and was told to come back that afternoon. That afternoon, when I came back, Delphine seemed really stressed out. She said, "I only have a minute, but come in and sit down." She had Navigo metro passes in her hand. They're like plasticized cards with your picture on them, and you add funds to them every month. I wanted to reach into the pile and find mine, but Delphine said they were short on funds this month, and no, I wasn't getting a metro pass.

I reminded her how often she'd promised I would get one for sure in February, but she just said, "I know, I'm sorry."

I explained how bad my feet hurt, and reminded her of the note from Dr. Schwartz and showed it to her again. I told her I needed to go to Saint-Ouen to look for work and I really was close to getting a job, but I needed to ride the metro because it was too far to continue walking. She just said, "I'm sorry, there are other women with health issues who need the passes too, and they've been here longer than you."

She said she would see if it would be OK to give me a few tickets, but the bottom line was no month-long metro pass.

I'd really been counting on that pass, and she'd reassured me many times I would get one. I rushed out of the office and went upstairs to my room. Social workers are supposed to enable us, not disable us, but I felt many times they were disabling me. Now I could see how so many of these women had gotten stuck in Malmaison for so long, and why many of them had given up. If you don't have a metro pass, it's not likely you'll be able to find work, and without work you can't leave the shelter. It made no sense. Isn't that what shelters are for? To help you get back on your feet?

I did realize later that it wasn't Delphine's fault. She did want to help me and the other women, she just didn't have the resources to do it. It must be very frustrating to be in Delphine's shoes. Later she explained that the women eligible for health care got a discount on their Navigo metro pass and that was pretty much all of them. She told me I should apply, but I had to wait till I had been in France three months.

Health care in America is very different. If you're not Bill Gates or Paris Hilton or from some rich family in Connecticut, and you don't have one of a select few privileged jobs, there's most likely no health care for you in America. Most jobs won't include it, or if they do, you'll have to pay the cost out of your salary.

Very rarely an employer will pay up to half the cost of your insurance plan, but you still usually pay around two hundred dollars a month, and that's if you're a healthy, young, single woman with no dependents. And there are only certain doctors and hospitals you can go to, and dental and vision coverage cost extra. They all have long waiting periods and co-payments for everything, twenty-five to fifty dollars for every doctor's appointment and every medication, and if you have to go to the emergency room, it's usually over a hundred dollars.

If you don't have health insurance, you can't walk in the door of most clinics and hospitals. If you have an accident or fall ill or need an operation, you're in big trouble. And you're going to hesitate before calling an ambulance because the base rate is $1,000 to $1,500 dollars, and they charge extra for certain meds and procedures, given en route. And a lot of emergency rooms won't treat you, or they'll just send you on to another hospital or emergency clinic.

Not in France—everyone who has the legal right to live in France gets free health care. Isn't that a better system than the one in America? Maybe America is the wealthiest country because its citizens pay so much for everything they have.

I was lucky; a few months before I left America, a nurse I met working through the nursing agency gave me the name and address of a free clinic in Gresham, Oregon: Good News Health Clinic. A lot of so-called free clinics don't accept new patients because the clinics are so few and far between. But this nurse explained that "Dr. Bob," as they nicknamed him, would never turn anyone away. So whenever I was ill, with flu, high-blood pressure, or whatever, I went to Dr. Bob. He worked long, hard hours, and he made an arrangement with a local pharmacy to give big discounts for any prescription with his name on it.

That was the only way I could afford my blood pressure medicine, but I still couldn't afford my cholesterol and gallbladder meds. Many of the people that worked there were volunteers because this was a true charity: They worked on donations. Sometimes I would arrive at eight in the morning and wouldn't be seen till four in the afternoon, but it was OK because everyone was always so kind. They had the same mentality as the people of Saint-Eustache: How may we be of service to you?

Then of course, in France there are free schools and free universities. Amazing! Don't even get me started. France has free daycare, preschool, primary, middle, and high schools, and of course universities—all free—wow!

And the vacation time—unbelievable. In America, again, if you are one of the few privileged employees, you get maybe ten days vacation a year, but it doesn't have to be guaranteed. The United States is the only advanced economy in the world that does not guarantee its workers paid vacation. In France they get eleven national holidays and five weeks vacation a year.

It's astounding. Most Americans would be thrilled to have what French people take for granted, and number one is health care. They enjoy the privilege of free medical insurance and affordable medication. It's based on your income: the less you make, the less you pay. For example, the cholesterol medicine I couldn't afford in America because it was over 250 U.S. dollars a month would never cost more than twenty euros in France, and that's if you're in the highest income bracket. And there are reasonable co-payments for most medical exams and hospitalizations, and operations for less than $1,000 if you need them—yes, that's really what I said. I know all of this is incomprehensible to the average American citizen, and at first it was to me too. Working in the health-care field for many years in America, I have seen many people lose everything—their homes, cars, jobs, savings—plus get into debt and ruin their credit because they owe $300,000 for an operation to save their life or the life of their child or spouse. That would never happen in France.

⚜ ⚜ ⚜

That night I hunted down the piece of paper Olivia had given me with her phone numbers on it, and I went down to the office and asked to use the phone, because I had no credit on the phone Djamila had lent me. But they wouldn't let me because one of her numbers began with 06, a French cell phone, and the other was 03, the eastern regions of France. I guess she lived in a suburb of Paris, and they only let you call 01 numbers from the office in Malmaison.

I knew they would let me use the phone at the Emmaus office in Saint-Ouen, so I begged Aicha to sneak me onto the metro the next morning and rode up there. I called Olivia and told her,

"I can't walk to Saint-Ouen several times a week to look for work, so if you think some kind of article can get me a metro pass, then I'm up for it." She said she would call me right back—in France, even if you have no credit on your phone, you can still receive calls; you just can't make them.

She called back after about ten minutes and said she had just received a message that a woman at the weekly supplement of *Le Monde,* the most important French daily newspaper, was interested in the story. She was all excited and said she'd been hoping to get *Elle* magazine interested—that made me laugh, me in *Elle* magazine! This woman, Pascale, worked at the weekend magazine, *Le Monde 2,* and that could be even better. She said Pascale wanted to know more about me before deciding whether to do an article, so she asked if she could give her my number.

I agreed. I didn't know what kind of magazine *Le Monde 2* was. I thought it would be like a little black-and-white newspaper supplement, but that was OK.

Pascale called me right back and we talked on the phone for about ten minutes, then made an appointment to meet at metro Châtelet.

Pascale was a really bright woman, with short hair and a kindness about her—kind but businesslike. She brought some copies of *Le Monde 2* with her, and when I saw what it looked like, this nice color magazine, I thought, *Wow, this is a big deal.* She took me to a nice restaurant, the first sit-down restaurant in Paris I ever got to walk into, sit down, and eat in, unless you count McDonalds.

I had sautéed mussels and a big green salad and dessert, and I ate every bit of it. It was pretty funny: She asked me what I wanted to drink, and I said, "coffee," and she very gently told me that in France you don't ever drink coffee with your food, not unless it's breakfast. You drink coffee after the meal.

Pascale spoke great English and she seemed really interested, so I told her my story. And we did have coffee, after the meal. She said she was interested in hearing more. She wanted to come to Malmaison and see where I was staying.

Then Olivia called and wanted to take some more photographs. I never have been comfortable in front of the camera, but Olivia was very kind and patient. She said she wanted a photo of me someplace where I went a lot, and I said that would be the Louvre, because I went there all the time. So we took the metro, and it was a little chilly. There are always people around the Louvre, and one of the gypsy women came up and tried to do the ring trick with Olivia. I told her no and then I explained the whole thing, and she burst out laughing. She said, "I've lived in France half my life and I didn't know that trick."

After the Louvre we walked onto a nearby bridge and Olivia took more photos. Then she apologized and said she should have taken pictures of me in my room at Malmaison before we left. So we headed back there on the metro, and when she'd finished taking photos, she asked if I needed anything. I immediately said contact-lens solution, tampons, and of course, metro tickets. So, we walked over to a pharmacy and she bought me a box of tampons and a bottle of contact-lens solution, which was really great because I had been making my own saline solution—just dissolving salt in water—since I didn't have any money, and I got an eye infection a couple of times. That was very kind of her, and I really appreciated it.

One of the photos Olivia took was of my feet in the old Z-CoiL boots I was wearing, and they were just about falling apart. There was a gummy bear right beside them, and a cigarette butt. I didn't even notice her taking that picture, but when I saw it printed out, I felt like it just about summed me up at that moment of my life.

And on the way back to Malmaison, I saw some fruit left over from the street market, like it wasn't worth packing back up into the van because it wasn't fresh enough to sell. Since I was in town all day and missed lunch, I was hungry. There were a couple of apples, hardly bruised at all, and some red balls covered with a kind of stiff green hair and big lumpy green fruit with spikes on it like dinosaur skin. I didn't know how I would eat that and it smelled kind of funky, but I picked up the apples, and they were good.

It ended up being April before I got enough money together for a metro pass.

13

The Grace of France

On February 10, my ninety-day permission to be in France as a tourist was used up. Hanging around Agora as much as I did, I knew what that meant: I was an illegal. I could be deported, and it was the strangest thing—I no longer wanted that to happen. I didn't feel like there was anything in America to go back to.

I had no place left to live, and no personal belongings, but that didn't seem so significant any longer. I also knew that in a few weeks my certification as a nursing assistant would be due, and if I didn't have the seventy-five dollars to renew it, then I would lose it, and I'd have to go back to class all over again to requalify before I could work.

How was I going to pay for the classes? And where would I stay, in a homeless shelter? Even if they have homeless shelters in Oregon, would it take me two or three months of living on the street to get into one? There were always a lot of homeless people on the street in Portland.

I don't know how the shelters work when you're homeless in America, but I know for sure that the street in any American city is a lot more violent than in Paris because guns are legal and everywhere. The place I lived with Chloe in Portland wasn't a bad neighborhood, it was actually fairly average, but somebody got knifed or shot pretty regularly. There was a convenience store nearby and it seemed like every week somebody was pulling a gun on a guy or smashing a window.

In Paris that doesn't happen, because guns are illegal. You can walk into a grocery store and leave your backpack by the door unattended, and when you've done your shopping and paid for your groceries, your backpack is right there waiting for you, untouched. You walk down avenue de Choisy many times of day, and there'll be a truck parked outside some restaurant; the guy will leave the truck wide open, with the keys in it and the engine running, while he does his delivery. In America the stuff would be stolen out of the truck or the truck itself would be stolen.

When I was walking the streets at night, a number of times the thought came to me: If that guy had a knife or a gun, or he was angry enough or crazy enough, I could be dead. I've worked in hospital emergency rooms, so I've seen what a knife or a gun can do to you. I figured, if I was on the street in America, someone would have pulled a gun or a knife on me, and I probably would have been raped or worse.

Now I knew about another world outside of America, and sometimes I liked that world a lot. I felt like living in France could be even better than living in the United States, at least for a while. People in France seemed to work less hours, and they seemed less driven by the need to make more money and buy more stuff. It seemed like I could learn from them and even if I lived cheaply, maybe I could have a better quality of life in France. Thanks to Malmaison—and to Francois—at least I had a place to stay over here.

February 10 was also the day I was supposed to leave Malmaison, because theoretically they only gave me a month when they let me back in, though they said it could be extended to ninety days. I knew that it wasn't that big a deal: at Malmaison they're not going to throw you out on the street if you can't find a job and a place to stay. I knew they wouldn't put me back out there, at least not in the winter, and judging from how long some of the women had been staying there, probably not ever. Maybe the shelter on rue Vulcan would've thrown me out, but not Malmaison.

❖ ❖ ❖

Pascale kept calling with questions, and she came out to Malmaison and interviewed me again. She wanted to talk in private, so she suggested we sit in the bedroom. Alice was there taking a nap, so Pascale asked her if it was OK if we sat there and talked. Alice said it was fine and went back to sleep.

Pascale was looking at my paperwork when Alice started snoring. Sometimes she snored loud, but not all the time, mostly when she was very tired, and I probably did too. Pascale said, "Oh my God, is it like that all night?" I said sometimes it was, but I told her that Alice was very kind, so it was OK, she was a good roommate. Pascale didn't write anything down, so I didn't think anything more about it.

She told me she was planning to write a big article. I asked Pascale, "Why me? Most of these women have been homeless far longer than me, and I'm sure some of them have lived through worse things than I have."

Pascale said yes, maybe, but I was American, that was the difference. She said if I was from almost any other country, *Le Monde 2* probably wouldn't be interested in doing the article.

I still didn't get it. I was so used to thinking that being born in America was such a huge disadvantage, an obstacle to getting help. I didn't understand that now it was suddenly becoming a huge advantage, that my situation was exceptional or newsworthy.

⚜ ⚜ ⚜

They had a new social worker and French teacher at Agora. She was a beautiful dark-skinned woman with short, dark hair. Her name was Margrete, but we called her Marg. She spoke English, Russian, and of course, French. She was usually very kind, but they would frequently pull her out of class to work another area of Agora.

The class was supposed to be twice a week, and I was still broke with no meal ticket. When I had a French lesson or an appointment in the center of town, there was no way to get back to Malmaison for lunch. So I would put bread in my pockets at breakfast or pack some leftovers and eat that, but I had to be careful of food poisoning.

One time a Croatian guy in my French class said he would show me the place he ate, near Notre Dame. It looked like a normal restaurant, but there was a crowd of men outside, and even by street standards they looked rough. A bunch of them smelled bad and some of them were real dirty and reeked of alcohol. I felt a strong presence of wolves.

They were only letting you in to eat if you already had a ticket from standing in line earlier that morning. Then a guy came to the door to give out more tickets, and the crowd rushed over to him. It was like being in the mosh pit at a rock concert, and I was right in the middle of them. Two guys beside me began fighting over a ticket. Even though what the wolves wanted wasn't me, I felt the need to immediately remove myself from the situation.

I started to leave, but the Croatian guy said, "It's OK," and he showed the ultimate act of compassion, and gave me his ticket. I waited to be sure that he got another one before I went in. Everyone was crammed together at long tables, but the food was really good and fresh, unlike the frozen, prepackaged homeless food. There was stew with big chunks of lean, tender, flavorful beef, rice, and as much fresh bread and sweet rolls as you wanted. They even gave you a piece of chocolate after your meal.

When the man sitting on my left was finished with his lunch, he sincerely smiled at me and tried to give me his chocolate. I said, no, it's OK, but he insisted, saying he didn't like chocolate; however, the chocolate-covered sweet roll sticking out of his bag suggested otherwise. My stomach was full and my heart was warm as I shook his hand and kindly thanked him: another random act of compassion.

These men may look and smell rough on the outside, but once you sit down and eat a meal with them, you see them in a whole new light. You look past physical form and see the compassionate, kind-hearted people that some of them can be. They're not all wolves and some of the ones that are, they're like domesticated wolves—they're just trying to survive.

Clearly none of them had meal tickets from social workers either. At that moment, I began to truly understand what Mother Teresa used to say, "Each one of them is Jesus in disguise."

⚜ ⚜ ⚜

A new supervisor arrived at Malmaison, so I went to meet him and ask about getting a Navigo metro pass. He was real busy and wouldn't make an appointment with me, so I ended up writing him a letter in English, because I was told he spoke some English and at that moment I wasn't able to write in French. I told him that I really didn't want to mooch off the French system. I didn't say this, but a lot of the women around me really did seem like they were kind of working the system a bit, and I was afraid I was being denied a metro pass because they thought I was like that.

I told him about all of the appointments I had, spread around town, and that I was going out every day, all day long. I was trying really hard to find a job and get things straightened out, but when I'm walking, two appointments can fill a whole day. I had to struggle to get back in time for dinner, and sometimes I couldn't make it, because if I got in after seven, I didn't eat.

There were days I'd leave Malmaison when the doors opened at six in the morning to make an eight o'clock appointment at Châtelet, and sometimes it would be after eight in the evening by the time I walked back to Malmaison. I told him he could check the documents—we had to sign out and give them our card every time we left Malmaison, and when we returned they would sign us in and take our card—I was pulling on all the resources I could, but I had to get around town in order to do that, so could he please just help with a metro pass for one or two months.

He never came through with a Navigo metro pass, but when I left, he was giving me ten tickets a week. It wasn't much, because some days if I had two or three appointments, so I could go through four or five tickets in a day, but it was a break. It meant I could walk some and use the metro some.

⚜ ⚜ ⚜

It had been a while since I'd hung out at the women's group at Montesquieu, so one afternoon I headed over just to see who was around and say hi. It wasn't really any kind of group, just a warm space where you didn't have to fight the wolves off, and if you didn't have any money, you could still sit and drink coffee or tea, because it was free.

Things were getting kind of complex for Chex: She was fighting with Mathilde. Mathilde was a very short woman and not mentally stable at all. I don't say that in a mean way; like I said, you can't begin to understand how bad it is out there if you haven't been on the street yourself. But Mathilde was truly in her own reality, and sometimes it was a pretty weird and angry place.

For instance, one day the washing machine at Montesquieu wasn't working and she just lost it and started yelling and scream-ing at the top of her lungs in the street. She was obviously in a lot of pain—pain causes anger. I didn't see her often when I slept at Montesquieu; she wasn't a regular like Marie. But she was always there on weekday afternoons, two to five, for the women's group, and sometimes she would just sit there, talking to herself for hours.

So, one day at Agora, Mathilde got mad at Chex—she could just flare up sometimes—and I wasn't there, but the upshot was Chex got thrown out of Agora for a while, and I guess she wasn't hang-ing out much at Montesquieu because Mathilde was always there.

I went out to try and find her, but she wasn't over by the Jardin des Halles in her usual place. In the middle of all this, I got a phone call on my cell from a woman who spoke English. She said she worked for a telemarketing center in Issy-les-Moulineaux and asked if I could come in and interview for a job.

I said sure, and she gave me a date and time, just a few days away.

⚜ ⚜ ⚜

The job interview was in Issy-les-Moulineaux, which is a suburb outside Paris, but it wasn't far from Malmaison. I could get there on the tram and then walk maybe thirty minutes from the tram stop. There were two people doing the interview—Olivier, who was the boss, and the Asian woman I'd spoken to on the phone.

It was a group interview, so I was there with a couple of other people: a lady from Germany and an American gentleman. We ended up working on the U.S. team together. They said they were look-ing for people with life experience, not particular qualifications, and what they wanted were native speakers of various languages.

Basically, if they called you in for the interview, that meant they liked your résumé; they asked you a couple of questions and you pretty much had the job, at least for a trial period.

They explained what it was about: They did telemarketing all over the world for international companies, like travel agencies and companies selling time-shares. The customers didn't always have to buy something; often we would call and offer a free two-day trip if they came to a seminar. Many of the customers were happy to go to a two-hour seminar in exchange for a free trip, so you'd dial the American number that came up on the computer, ask to speak to the person listed, and then tell him or her a bunch of info from a script.

You needed to keep it really quick because you needed to get three trips an hour—at least, that was the goal for this particular one—and if you didn't do enough, you were fired. But if they kept you on, you got a CDD, which is a kind of job contract, and they said they would file for papers on my behalf, so I could work legally in France, and live there.

So, I got the job, and my tentative start date was about three weeks away.

⚜ ⚜ ⚜

Pascale gave me the number of a woman at the U.S. Embassy and told me to call her. She said this woman would give me some help. I called, but she seemed kind of judgmental and stiff. I told her what had happened when I went to the embassy before Christmas, and she told me she couldn't make head or tail of my story. She said the embassy flew people back to America if they ran out of money when they were traveling in Europe. She said it was a loan for repatriation, and when they got you back to the United States they kept your passport till you paid the money back

She offered to fly me back to Portland, and she said again that they would take my passport till I paid all the money back for the ticket.

When I was about to freeze to death on the street, I would have jumped at this offer. But by this time, I was safe in a women's shelter and had been offered a job with a CDD contract.

I explained to the woman that in America, I'd be on the street. I had nothing left. Even my nursing certification was gone now, because I didn't have the money to renew it. I told her I would never survive on the street in America because there are too many guns and knives. She never offered any assistance with that. She just told me the embassy would get me the plane ticket back to Portland and take away my passport, and I would not be allowed to reapply for another passport until I'd paid all the money back.

Oh, and she warned me that sometimes it can be difficult to get another passport after this kind of thing happens. She explained there were cases that were never resolved, and the people were never allowed to leave America again: they couldn't get another passport.

⚜ ⚜ ⚜

The idea of being held hostage in the country I was born in just didn't appeal to me. I knew that even at my former rate of pay, it would have taken me months of working double shifts to pay them back for the ticket, more if they charged interest, and in America they charge interest for everything.

I would have to start from nothing, retrain and get recertified for my old job as a CNA. That alone would have taken three to five months. Then I would have to find a job and a place to stay, make the normal bills, and pay back a huge debt for an embassy plane ticket. I felt like it could take me years, and what if they never let me have another passport?

And there were also the refugees; I couldn't stop thinking about them. America leads the way in an unconscious war that destroys the countries they were born in and makes them homeless, and France graciously opens her arms and takes them in. I almost felt like if I went back to America while the war continued, I would be condoning it.

Suddenly America didn't seem like a better alternative.

At that moment, in France, I had a job and a safe place to stay. In America, I would be homeless and jobless. I would be on the street again, but the wolves would have weapons, and I probably wouldn't be able to escape their grasp.

So I made the logical choice. I would stay here, work hard, and save up, and if I wanted to go back, after the war ended, I could pay for my own ticket when that time came.

⚜ ⚜ ⚜

A few days later, the social workers at Montesquieu had planned a big outing for us. We were supposed to go to the Louvre, and I was so excited because I had never seen the inside, but for some reason we ended up going to the Musée d'Orsay instead; still, that was really cool too.

I spent a long time looking at the chair in Van Gogh's *Bedroom in Arles*, and I remembered what Eckhart Tolle says in *A New Earth:*

> *"Van Gogh looked and looked and looked at it and really felt the beingness of the chair. Then he sat in front of the canvas and took up the brush. The chair itself would have sold for the equivalent of a few dollars. The painting of that same chair today would fetch in excess of $25 million."*

I looked up, and there was *Starry Night Over the Rhone*. It's always been one of my favorite paintings. When I was in my twenties, I had a poster-sized replica of it on my wall, so to see the actual painting right there in front of me was amazing. The detail of each brushstroke can only really be appreciated with the actual painting right in front of you, and I don't believe I will ever own a replica again.

Then I went and stood behind the huge glass clock and thought about how many nights I had walked along the river, looking up at it, wondering how to get home. The social worker had to come up and tug my arm to get me to come away.

14

Malmaison

Pascale called and told me the article was running in *Le Monde 2* that weekend, February 22, and she had sent a courier over to Malmaison with some copies for me. I was at Agora, so I walked back to Malmaison to take a look, but when I asked they said there were no packages for me anywhere.

So the next morning I walked to the *Le Monde* building on boulevard Auguste-Blanqui to pick up a magazine. I asked for Pascale at the reception desk, but the woman there looked at me weirdly and said she wasn't there. I tried to explain to her that I just wanted a copy of the magazine. A man came up who spoke English and asked, "Where are you from?" I told him America, and he smiled and said, "I'll be right back."

He walked across the room and picked up a magazine. On his way back, he showed the woman at the desk the magazine and she looked up at me and smiled. He brought it over and showed me there was a long article, several pages, with two pictures of me, and a lot of incomprehensible text. It was the weirdest feeling to see pictures of myself in a magazine.

I put the magazine in my coat pocket and walked into Agora for my French lesson. In the middle of class, a social worker said there was a French man on the phone asking for me, and it was something about a newspaper article. It was the blond social worker who turned me away from the office that first time I had the appointment with Suzanne.

She asked the French teacher to translate and ask me if I wanted her to take a message, and I said, "Yes, please," and thanked her. After class, the teacher asked me what all this was about, what newspaper article? I pulled the magazine out of my coat pocket and showed her, and she asked if she could photocopy it.

When I called the guy back, he spoke really great English. He said his name was Julien, and he'd read the *Le Monde 2* article and wanted to help me, so we made an appointment to meet at Châtelet the next morning.

When I got back to Malmaison, people were acting really strange. They were talking together, ignoring me, or throwing me black, hostile looks. The tension was building, especially when everyone was together at dinner. I guess Hind intercepted my package from Pascale when the courier brought it over; she was always signing for things and acting like she ran the place.

Over the course of the weekend, it seemed like pretty much everyone heard about the article, and they were angry. It was like a big shift in energy, and I wasn't sure what was going on, but I felt the tension increasing. People had pretty much always been warm and positive to me at Malmaison, but the atmosphere was becoming so harsh and negative now.

There was a woman who had lived in Australia and who spoke English well; she looked like a transsexual—you'd really swear she was a man; she had a rough voice and she had very male-looking features and wore a blond wig, which she was always curling and teasing. She was a little odd, but she could be really nice: One day she said she'd teach me how to tease my hair up too, but after the article appeared, she swung cold and wouldn't speak to me.

I would walk into a room and everyone would stop talking. Aicha had always been kind to me, but now she wasn't anymore. One time I walked into a room and Aicha said—first in English, and then in French, "Oh, it's OK, she doesn't understand French," and they all started talking again. All of a sudden it was like Aicha and Hind were joined at the hip: They were always together, whispering and pointing and staring at me.

Hind and another woman, Tourya, were talking about how all American women sleep around, and since I was American, that meant I was a slut, and Alice had just pretty much disappeared. She wasn't sleeping in our room anymore. I'd go back upstairs and see she had come by and changed her clothes or left something on the bed, but clearly she was avoiding me.

Pakistan saw how uneasy I was, and she came over and talked to me. She said the women there were stressed, and I shouldn't take it personally, sometimes life is a struggle. I knew her life had been difficult, and that even with a part-time job she didn't have much money, because she had to pay a little rent to Malmaison. She hugged me and said God would look after me, he would bless me. She said she knew that, she could feel it. She was very kind, and that meant more to me than words can say.

⚜ ⚜ ⚜

At first I thought the violence on the street was primarily against women, but I have learned the men also suffer incredible acts of violence. If someone sees you have something they want, and you refuse to give it up, they will often attack.

It could be something as simple as a jacket or bag. Perhaps it's the only jacket you have to keep you warm, and the bag has all your papers inside: ID, birth certificate, legal citizenship, work info, etc. So you guard them with your life: to give them up would jeopardize your livelihood and your survival.

Please use empathy here, not sympathy: The wolves attack you repeatedly over a long period of time. You learn to see them coming, and you know they are going to attack and try to take your means of survival. Perhaps when you see them approach, you start to initiate the attack as a defense mechanism, but remember, you have been broken down to your core.

Your primary goal is to survive. You get beat up on a regular basis for years, and you are able to survive by fighting back. What you first viewed as violent behavior has slowly become normal behavior and you subconsciously start rebuilding yourself with your new *normal* behavior.

This conditioned behavior—fighting equals survival—takes you over, so whenever you're threatened, you fight. It's what you have learned, what has subconsciously been instilled in your mind. You go from being attacked to starting the attack whenever you feel threatened in any way, and maybe you're not even conscious of it.

⚜ ⚜ ⚜

I went over to Chex's tent and we went for a walk in the park. I just wanted to be with someone I knew wouldn't judge me. Then I heard a familiar voice say, "Hey." I turned around and it was Francois. I hadn't seen him in quite a while, but he explained he'd been in a fight recently and his phone had gotten broken. He had a pretty big lump on his head and a new phone number, so I believed him.

Francois told me he'd been working on a truck at the garage and he heard some guy on the radio talking about the article in *Le Monde 2*. I was like, it's on the radio? And Francois said, "Yes, and by the description, I knew it was you, so I came here to find out if you were OK."

I was very glad to see him again, and it felt good that he cared. We went out for a walk down by the river, and I told him all about what was going on at Malmaison. I asked him if he was still at Montesquieu. He said he still didn't have enough money together to rent a place, but he had a tent.

We both stopped walking and started laughing, because he had been so against tents when I asked him to help me find one, back before Christmas. It was like he changed his mind after trying to help me.

He said he had a good place to set the tent up—it was kind of like a balcony above the Forum des Halles mall, right between the offices of the nonprofit organization that also let some people store their stuff and the Restaurant du Cœur office. It was also the same place I helped drop off Stéphanie's suitcases. It was like a concrete platform, but it had an overhang, so it was somewhat protected from the weather.

He said the tent was easily big enough for two, and he had a couple of sleeping bags, so I could come there and stay with him anytime I wanted. I said, "I have my sleeping bag and you have yours, right?" and he said "Yes." It would get me away from the situation at Malmaison, maybe just for a day or two, and give things time to calm down.

Francois was always kind and respectful to me. One time in the Jardin des Halles he'd tried to kiss me and I just said no, and that was OK: He put his hands up and backed away politely. So I didn't think he was trying to take advantage of me. I trusted him and felt safe when he was around. I just thought he was being kind, but I said, "No, thank you, I'm OK for right now."

⚜ ⚜ ⚜

The next morning I met Julien in a café, one of those big French bistros where they keep newspapers on a long wooden stick for people to read while they're drinking coffee. He'd brought a file with him where he'd printed out different resources from the English-speaking community in France. He also brought an incredible bag of stuff: food, maps, metro tickets, deodorant, body wash, and also a notebook and a pen. He said I should start writing down everything I could remember about what had happened to me. He worked at a theater, and he said he thought I should write a book. He gave me his cell number and told me to call any time I needed anything.

It was noon when Julien said he had to go to work, so I walked straight over to Chex's tent and I told her to come with me to the park, that I had a surprise. We sat down on a bench and I opened up the incredible bag. There were two pieces of roast chicken, green beans from Monoprix, cheese, and cookies. We had a picnic, the most amazing picnic of my life. I love roast chicken, but it never tasted as good as it did that day.

We ate till we were so full, and then we split the rest. Chex was so thrilled and grateful she almost cried.

⚜ ⚜ ⚜

I took the metro back to Malmaison with my new metro tickets, but when I got back, I couldn't bear to expose myself to the atmosphere in the dining hall. So I picked up my food and took it upstairs to the room I shared with Alice. This wasn't allowed, although I'd seen women eating in their rooms all the time.

But Djamila followed me up to the room and kept shaking her head and saying, "No, forbidden, *interdit*," and then she would point downstairs. She was speaking roughly to me, and I was letting the emotions get to me; my eyes started welling up with tears.

One of the French girls who lived across the hall came in. She was young, slim, and very pretty, and she translated that it was forbidden to bring food up to the bedroom. I explained that many of the other women did it every day.

Djamila said, "I have never seen them," and the French girl was very understanding; she told me that I could come downstairs and sit with her tonight and tomorrow for dinner.

The next morning I got up early and went down to the dining hall at six thirty to roll some cigarettes before breakfast was ready at seven. One of the employees, Tourya, was there. She had always been nice to me, and we even danced together on New Year's Eve, but now she told me to get out. I said it was OK, I wasn't expecting coffee or anything, no *mangé*, but suddenly she was angry with me, and she pointed her finger to the door and started yelling. She kept yelling at me till I left the dining hall.

When I stood in line at lunch, another woman started shouting at me because when she moved her bag of food in the fridge, something spilled out of my bag. I was still saving food and walking it down to place d'Italie for the homeless people every two or three days. After going a few days without food, I still couldn't bring myself to just throw good food away.

She kept yelling and yelling, like she was about to explode, and I tried to defuse the whole thing, so I said, "It's OK, nobody died, I'll clean it up." The Arab man who worked there laughed and she kept yelling at me while I cleaned it up. When I sat down, everyone seemed angry. The tension was so thick you could cut it with a knife.

I figured the best option was to remove myself from the situation, so I picked up my food and went and sat on a chair just outside the dining hall, but I could still hear them talking about me. The Arab man came out of the kitchen and saw me, and he turned the radio way up so I wouldn't have to hear it. He was always kind to me.

But at dinner that night, the nice young French girl was gone. I didn't want a repeat of lunch, so I took my food and put it in the fridge. I figured I could come downstairs and eat it later. But when I was heading down the hall to my room, the new supervisor said, "Wait right there, we need to talk." I thought maybe something had happened about a metro pass, but he had a copy of the *Le Monde 2* article and said, "A lot of the women are very upset."

I still hadn't read the article because it was in French. I could only make out a word here or there, and at this point no one had taken the time to sit down and read it to me. So I asked him why they were upset, and he showed me, this paragraph here, and he handed it to me. He was like, go ahead, read it, you'll see.

Like I could manage to read a long magazine article in French! I reminded him I knew little French, and I asked him if he could just explain what was going on.

He told me the women were saying that I told the journalist my roommate snored like a freight train. They said it was disrespectful, and that I had said bad things about Alice and about them, although actually there was nothing about anyone else in the article, only about Alice, and I didn't say it.

I didn't tell Pascale anything bad. She walked into the bedroom and heard Alice snoring. I assumed what she had witnessed was off the record because she didn't write anything down. I hadn't said anything bad about anyone, not even Hind, and they took what Pascale wrote out of context, they created all of this negative drama, and now they were hurt and angry. I guess it didn't really matter what Pascale wrote; they thought the magazine article should have been about them.

I tried to explain to the director what had happened, and that I hadn't said a bad word about any of them, but he didn't want to listen. He said I was disrupting the whole household and that everyone was in an uproar because of me. He raised his voice and was speaking very firmly and harshly. He sounded angry about the situation, angry at me.

I decided in an attempt to keep the peace I should remove myself from the situation.

"Do you know what is better than charity, fasting, and prayer? Keeping the peace and good relations among people, as quarrels and bad feelings destroy mankind."
　　　　　　　　　　　　　　　　　—Muslim hadith

So I took a shower, got dressed, and put some stuff in my backpack. Then I went downstairs to the dining hall and got my dinner out of the fridge. I followed protocol—signed the book and turned in my card—and I reported I was going to spend the night with a friend, and then I walked out.

I walked back in to Châtelet, to the place above the Forum des Halles, at 101 rue Rambuteau, where Francois had set his tent up. As I walked, I remember thinking it was kind of ironic: Francois was the kind man who stood up to the social worker and got me off the street into the shelter. Now I was making the choice to leave the shelter and go back to the street with him, but he had a tent this time, and I knew he would protect me from the wolves, and he always treated me with respect.

15

Back on the Street

Francois was hanging out with some friends inside, and they only let certain people in the office, so I had to wait a little while on the stairway at 101 rue Rambuteau. It was about nine forty-five when Francois came out to set up his tent. He was so comforting—he hugged me and was sincerely happy to see me, and he put me at ease. He showed me the two sleeping bags, and told me again, "This one is yours," and I felt so much better once I saw him.

Ever since the day when he stood up for me with Suzanne and basically saved my life, I had seen him in a new light. I trusted him, and I knew he would stand up for me and protect me from the wolves if needed.

He gave me the nicer sleeping bag and we lay down to sleep. He kissed me goodnight and I reminded him, "My sleeping bag and yours." He said yes and respectfully backed away into his bag, but when I zipped the bag up, it wasn't very thick. It was a really cold night and the cement was cold and hard to sleep on, very different from the lumpy mattress on the bed at Malmaison. The tent was one of those two-person pop-up tents that Médecins du Monde gives away, about twice the size of Chex's, so it didn't get as warm as hers did just from our body heat.

In the middle of the night I woke up shivering, so cold that I couldn't sleep. I woke up Francois and asked him to unzip his bag. He said, "No, this is my bag and that is your bag," and he smiled so I knew he was joking. Then I showed him we could zip the two bags together and that would keep our body heat in better. The rest of the night we were warm and we slept, just slept together, fully clothed. Again I felt safe with him.

The next morning Francois left to go to the garage where he worked, and I had a couple of appointments to go to. That evening I headed back to Malmaison and took a shower and changed my clothes, but I don't remember if I saw anybody. I knew Hind would be talking even worse about me now that I'd spent the night out, but I didn't care. I wasn't going to be sucked into their self-created drama anymore, because I had removed myself from the situation.

The place where Francois would set his tent up, 101 rue Rambuteau, was like a place where shipwrecks get cast up on shore, random and battered. There were about eight or nine people sleeping on the concrete roof area, which was up a flight of stairs from a Bodum shop selling fancy coffeemakers. It was windy and cold, but it was mostly protected from the rain. At night, after they closed the office, we, the shipwrecks, would set up. Francois had the only tent, and the agreement was that the tent had to be cleared up and stashed away when the office staff started coming in at seven in the morning. The others, who were all men, slept in their coats, blankets, or sleeping bags.

During the day, Francois stashed our stuff inside the office, and we would meet on the steps when he got back across town after work. He was working a split shift, so his days were long. He would bring me food when he could; he knew my favorites were salads, because they very seldom serve salads to homeless people, and gummy bears. You've got to understand how important food is when you're living on the street, especially in the winter. You burn a lot of extra calories keeping warm, but thanks to Francois, I didn't have to walk anymore.

Francois was making some money, I don't know how much, but he had a son to support. Once he went to the bank and got some money, he gave me thirty euros, and I bought cigarettes and a few groceries: a jar of peanut butter and chocolate spread, fresh bread, and of course sardines. Now, don't get the wrong idea. I don't love sardines, but they're cheap, healthy, nonperishable, easy to carry and eat, and with some bread they fill you up and keep you going.

Francois speaks four different languages. He is fluent in French and Arabic, but he also speaks a fair amount of English and Italian. He had a pocket French–English dictionary, similar to the one Aicha had. We used to look words up, and it got to be kind of fun.

His English was pretty good anyway, and my French started getting a little better, and we spent time talking, getting to know each other better. One time we were hanging out in Les Halles, watching the kids riding the big old merry-go-round, and he said maybe his next paycheck he'd have the money to buy me a ride.

I said I wanted to ride on the black horse with no tail, because nobody ever rode it, but he said no: "You ride in the carriage, like a princess."

Other times my feet were so painful I couldn't sleep, and he gave me foot rubs. They felt so good. It had been a long time since someone sincerely took care of me. When I would thank him, he'd say, "Always, every night."

⚜ ⚜ ⚜

We were growing much closer, but it was very cold, way too cold to take our clothes off, and there were people sleeping all around us. The two men who slept right by the tent would drink and be very loud till three or four in the morning. Francois would yell at them, "Shut up, I have to get up and go to work early in the morning," and they'd yell, "Stop complaining, at least you have a job!" So there was no privacy.

But between us there was a really good feeling, and our relationship was evolving.

I really didn't expect to become homeless and find a boyfriend, but Francois took his time. I didn't want to make love in a tent with a bunch of guys sleeping right outside, and he understood and was patient with me.

⚜ ⚜ ⚜

I was in the tent with Francois one night when he said he needed to go out to the magic toilet before they closed. I felt a very strong presence of a wolf nearby, and I asked him not to go, but he said he would be right back. After he left, the wolf started sniffing around the tent, pacing just like an animal. I could hear him breathing and I saw his shadow.

He kept pacing around the tent—he was all but panting—and then I realized I had overlooked one of my main rules for survival on the street: always have an escape route, never let yourself get cornered. I was trapped inside the tent, alone. I watched silently as his shadow moved toward the front of the tent, by the door.

Then he started to unzip the first door; both the zipper doors were closed, but there was no padlock. My heart felt like it was going to burst through my chest, and the hair was standing up on the back of my neck.

All of a sudden, I heard Francois yelling something in French, and the wolf moved away. Francois unzipped the door to make sure I was OK, and he kept yelling at the wolf. He got inside the tent and zipped both flaps shut and held me.

After a few moments, the wolf came back, pacing around the tent again. Francois pulled out a knife, and crouched at the door of the tent in attack position. He yelled out something in French that sounded like he meant it, and the wolf finally backed off.

Later, I was safe asleep in Francois's arms when I was awakened by a scream. Then it went quiet. Was I dreaming? I was starting to drift off to sleep again when I heard more screaming. It seemed to be coming from below us, maybe from the mall, which is closed at night, or the underground parking lot that was right underneath the stairwell.

It was a woman's voice, and at first she was just screaming, but then I heard the words: It was English, and she was screaming for help, shouting in a panic, "Help! No! Stop!"

The wolf found his victim, I thought. If Francois hadn't come back in time, it could have been me. The parking lot was heated; maybe this woman decided to go down there to get warm and she was trapped.

I shook Francois awake and explained what was happening. He told me it was too dangerous to go outside at that time of night; we didn't know how many attackers there were, and if he burst in they might beat him up and then get me. He said we didn't have a choice. I wanted to call the police, but I had no credit on my phone, and Francois's battery was dead. He went back to sleep, but I kept hearing the screaming, intermittently, in English; I was nauseous and terrified.

At about five in the morning, I heard what sounded like the police. There was controlled yelling in French, and then I heard what I thought sounded like clubs hitting someone. The screaming stopped.

⚜ ⚜ ⚜

It is vicious on the street, and not just in America, but in Paris too. I already knew that, but now I kept thinking about what the woman from the embassy told me. Paris is too dangerous for a woman alone, especially on the street, and she tried to persuade me to be repatriated.

She kept saying she knew what she was talking about, and if I had seen some of the stuff that came across her desk, about what happened to American women alone in Paris, I would change my mind. She repeated, "Paris is no place for a woman on her own."

I just kept it would be a lot worse in America because guns are legal, and I'm not sure how much difference this made, but I guess in a way I no longer felt like I was a woman completely on my own: there was Francois now.

16

Up Close and Personal with the Wolves

I started working at the telemarketing center at Issy-les-Moulineaux, and it was hard, especially on as little sleep as I was getting. I was calling people in America and trying to convince them if they went to a two-hour seminar about time-shares, they would get a free two-day trip to Las Vegas, Reno, or New York. But the people I spoke to seemed so hostile.

When they figured out that they wouldn't get the trip until after the seminar, nine times out of ten they would put the phone down, and often they'd throw in a few insults and some attitude as well. You see, in America, time is money, and everything revolves around money.

I was struggling to fill my quota, and the American guy I interviewed with was fired because his rate of completed seminars was too low. Mostly I felt the pressure of these people's attitudes, the hostility coming through the phone at me, and every day it made me appreciate France even more. But I was taking this aggressive behavior personally, so I was really resisting the work; I didn't like doing it and I was barely making the average of three an hour I was supposed to get.

But after a few weeks I started getting used to the job, and I stopped taking it personally. I would sit down at the desk in front of the computer and almost meditate for a moment before starting work. I reminded myself to stop resisting and to accept this moment fully. It was as if sometimes the job became a spiritual practice. My average went up to four, sometimes even five seminars an hour once I stopped resisting, and I made connections on the phone with some amazing people.

⚜ ⚜ ⚜

In the meantime, Julien called and took me to an association that sometimes helped women out, La Clairière. He explained my situation, and showed them a copy of my CDD contract at the telemarketing company. Julien explained how shook up I was about the wolf attack I recently overheard while sleeping in the tent, and they agreed to put me up in a hotel for a few nights.

They gave me a print-out of some hotels that rent by the month, so if I couldn't find an apartment right away I could go there. Then they called around and found a hotel over by Gare de l'Est for me to stay in temporarily.

I took the metro to Gare de l'Est and found the street on the map just a few blocks away. Underneath the address were two big doors. They were unlocked, so I went inside to look for the office. It opened up to a big courtyard, similar to the hostel I stayed at by Pont Marie when I first came to town.

There appeared to be four different buildings: A, B, C, and D. I went to each building looking for the hotel reception, but all of the doors were locked and I had to have a code or key to get inside.

I saw a door ajar with a man sitting inside, so I approached the door, and he said it wasn't the office, and I shouldn't be wandering around the courtyard alone. He appeared to be Spanish but spoke some English. He looked at the paper in my hand with the address and phone number on it, and shrugged. Then he told me to call the number on the paper.

There was no credit on the phone I was using, so I asked a woman with a cell phone to make the call for one euro. Then she saw it was an 01 number and said it would cost five euros. I didn't have that much, so I walked back toward the entrance. Then she said OK and made the call. The place I was supposed to be was a block further down the road. I gave her the one euro and she showed me where it was; there was no address at that door.

I gave the paper from La Clairière to the man at the counter. He appeared to be from India. He was nice, and he spoke some English. I checked in. The room was small but clean, and it had a toilet with a seat, a shower, and a TV. The window opened up to the courtyard I was in earlier with the four buildings. They appeared to be apartments. I heard every sound, as people would enter and leave through the courtyard.

The first night I didn't sleep much, and I missed Francois, but we agreed after hearing the wolf attack that this was best till I could move into an apartment.

⚜ ⚜ ⚜

A lot of people had emailed Pascale after the *Le Monde* 2 article came out, offering to help me. It seemed like they were genuinely concerned, but most of the time when I tried to take them up on an offer, like helping me with my French, I never heard from them again. Perhaps it was just communication: Maybe they didn't know enough English, and I was still looking for a dependable place to learn French with no money.

Still, there were a few amazing exceptions. One woman, Karen, was Franco-American and she suggested I go to the American Cathedral and ask for help. It was a nice building near the Alma Bridge, and I'd seen it before, but just never realized there was anything American about it. Priest Jonathan rode up on his bicycle; he was really kind and helpful, very easy to talk with and down-to-earth. He asked what brought me to Paris and listened as I explained the situation. Then he walked with me to a nearby tobacco store and bought twenty euros of credit for the phone I was using. After that we walked down to the metro station, and he bought *two* carnet of tickets—a carnet is ten tickets.

That was one of the kindest things anyone had done for me since I got stuck here. Priest Jonathan also explained they had a free lunch for people in need every Friday and he showed me where to sign up.

As I was leaving the Cathedral, I picked up a copy of FUSAC, and right there at the metro station George V, I started calling the ads for small apartments. I left a message for one of the ads in English; it was a small studio with an affordable price.

⚜ ⚜ ⚜

My second night at the hotel was very disturbing; around eleven thirty, I heard a woman screaming. At first I thought her boyfriend or husband was hitting her, or worse, but the screams went on intermittently till about five the next morning. I realized this was the second woman I'd heard being attacked in the last week, and like the first, she was screaming in English, "No! Stop! Please!"

I got up and found a guy who worked at the hotel and asked him to call the police. He said he already did, and that this happened every weekend, and if the woman willingly went into the apartment with the men, it was her fault. I couldn't believe it. No woman would go into an apartment knowing she was going to be attacked, and why didn't any of the neighbors call the police? Could they not understand her English? In America, everyone would have called 911, and the police would have been there in minutes.

The woman screamed, and the men hooted and hollered, "Oh là là! Do you like that?" and of course she screamed, "No! Please stop, you're hurting me!" But they didn't stop, they just turned the music up even louder. It was Indian or Arabic music. Then intermittently with the screams I would hear that musical tone from across the street at Gare de l'Est—*da-domp, da-domp*. It was the eeriest sound. To this day whenever I'm at a metro station where they play that musical tone, I hear the screams again, and it sends shivers up and down my spine.

In between the screams, the wolves began stumbling out of the building. One by one they left, then more screaming, then another wolf would leave. She continued begging them to stop. I heard two or three of them talking in the courtyard. They spoke a different language, it wasn't French or English, maybe Arabic, but with an accent I wasn't familiar with.

Around five in the morning, I heard a man escorting the victim out of the building into the courtyard. She was stumbling. The wolf escorting her spoke in English, and he told her to pick her feet up, they were almost there. She tried to talk, but her speech was very slurred now. I couldn't make out what she was saying, although all night her voice was very clear. Did they drug her? Or was she incapacitated and in shock from being gang-raped for six hours?

The man told her, in English, that she could sleep the rest of the night there by the door, even though it was now after five. It sounded as though he assisted her to the ground—I heard a body sliding down the wall, then a thump on the ground. This was happening right outside my window. I was horrified and nauseated, and again I remembered what the woman at the U.S. Embassy told me, Paris isn't safe for a woman alone.

I also remembered the offer I received at Gare de l'Est. Had this started as an offer like that? Did the woman enter the apartment several hours earlier cold and hungry, did she only want to eat and warm up? My first offer of food and warmth said nothing about sex; it was only if I wanted to spend the night that they expected sex.

I was very cold and hungry the night the men offered me a place to eat and warm up, but my instinct said no, it wasn't safe. This could have been me.

17

A Safe Place

I was more than ready to move into a little apartment, a safe place where the wolves couldn't touch me. I knew I had to get out of this hotel soon. It wasn't safe.

The morning after the latest wolf attack, I was on the outskirts of the 17th—the end of line 3 on the metro—on my way to a hotel that rented by the month, when my phone rang. It was a man who had placed an ad for a studio apartment in FUSAC returning my phone call. He spoke English well and explained he had been out of town and recently returned and got my message. He gave me the address of the apartment for rent; it was just outside Paris in a suburb called Montreuil. He said he could meet me there at two the next day.

I called Karen, the kind *Le Monde 2* reader who had been a wealth of information. I gave her the address of the apartment I was going to look at and asked about the neighborhood. She explained that a variety of cultures lived there, and she offered to meet me to look at the apartment and lease, if one was offered. Of course I took her up on her kind offer, expecting that if a lease was involved it would be in French.

Montreuil turned out to be a kind of funky neighborhood. It was very ethnic: Chinese restaurants alongside African and Arab grocery stores. It was great. Not far from there, at Porte de Montreuil, was a strange sort of market, like a flea market, where people just spread cloth on the sidewalk and sold a few beat-up plates, pots and pans, telephones, or just one pair of sneakers.

The apartment building was old but clean, and the stairs were endless, but when we got to the top there was a small room with a sofa bed, a sink, a small fridge, a little shower, and a toilet with a seat. The window didn't have a balcony, but it had a lovely wrought-iron railing, and the window shutters opened up like little French doors, just like the kind I used to look up at walking around place des Victoires at night, the kind I really liked. That was so cool.

We talked for a while with the owner. He was a kind man, I guess in his late thirties or early forties with shoulder-length dark curly hair. He agreed to take me on as a tenant for 460 euros a month, even though I barely had the money to give him for a three-month guarantee, thanks to my first paycheck and a very kind *Le Monde 2* reader. Francois loaned me the rest and the landlord said I could move in April 1. And I could have guests, sure, but no pets, and no permanent boyfriend; the apartment was too small for two people to live there all the time.

⚜ ⚜ ⚜

I talked to Francois, and he said he could stay with a friend for a couple of weeks. After that, someone he worked with was going back to Morocco to take care of his mother, who had become ill, and he had talked about subletting his room out to Francois while he was gone. Francois said the other roommates were Arab men and it wouldn't be appropriate for me to stay there, but it was fine for him.

The next night, I was waiting at the Louvre to meet Francois when a wolf approached. I felt his presence before I saw him, and it's my belief that being able to do that had saved me more than once. He asked if I was a tourist and talked about "the City of Love" and how he was here in town all by himself.

I said, "I have a boyfriend." He wanted me to walk with him, have coffee, blah blah blah. When I refused all the above, he took his hand and made aggressive sexual movements to himself, like he wanted me to do something sexual to him right there in the courtyard of the Louvre.

I was disgusted but also frightened at first, and then I remembered what Eckhart Tolle teaches in his books: Darkness can't survive in light, so you must learn how to become the light. I let my mind go quiet, and my body still, shoulders back, head up, spirit completely present. I looked the wolf directly in the eyes and I didn't say a word. He seemed confused and shook his head and started backing up. He looked straight into my eyes, and his expressions changed from aggressive to timid, then he jogged away and left the courtyard.

It's very difficult, for me anyway, to stay or be completely present in each moment, especially when I'm surrounded by a threatening, unconscious presence. That was the first time I was able to knowingly do this. It was another glimpse of the power of being present, truly present. Some glimpses are longer than others, and although I had gained a lot of awareness, I still had—and still have—a long way to go. I continue to become more and more aware of when I am resisting. Because I am aware of it, does that mean I can always accept and live in the present moment? It doesn't, not always, but I am aware that I need to do it, and therefore acceptance will come.

⚜ ⚜ ⚜

The first night at the apartment I wanted to be all by myself, and Francois was OK with that, so I carried my backpack up the seven flights of stairs and opened the door with my key. Inside, after I'd locked all three locks shut, I sat on the little sofa bed and looked around at my new place. The walls were bare, but the cupboards were full, not with food, but a full set of dishes and cutlery—well, two of everything, and as far as the rest of the apartment, it was just waiting to come to life.

I walked over to the French door–style windows and opened them up, and I leaned way out of them and looked down as the people walked by on the sidewalk below. I wondered if any of them were looking up, longing for a little apartment, with a little window like the one I was leaning out of. I wanted to yell down a word of encouragement just in case, but I refrained. I finally had a safe place of my own, just like I dreamed of on those long cold nights, a warm place, where the wolves couldn't touch me.

Epilogue

I wrote my father, sisters, and brother. I told them I forgave them, I would always love them, and I apologized for the misperceptions of the past. They almost seemed like a lifetime ago. They made their choices and I made mine. I didn't want to hurt anyone with this book, but I felt the reader needed to understand why I had no one to call. My father and his wife wrote back almost immediately. They said it was good to hear from me, and they loved me very much. It was very good to hear from them and I wrote them back immediately. We continue to exchange letters and catch up on the lost years.

What makes men become wolves? How are they created? What kind of horror do they have to live through, and what kind of pain do they have to endure, to make them start hurting innocent people? How many times do they have to get beat up and victimized themselves before all of the violence and pain builds up in them, to the point it has no place to go? But it has to get out, like a separate entity living inside; it temporarily takes possession of their form. It inflicts the pain and terror onto another being and then becomes dormant again until it's triggered by more pain and horror, like a bear hibernating in the winter. When conditions become optimal for feeding, it awakens the beast from within.

Is it possible to teach them how to deal with this pain, without inflicting it upon another being? Can we teach them about "the pain body," as Eckhart Tolle so eloquently puts it? Or would simply being put in a safe environment and being loved unconditionally and treated with respect be enough to make them realize that their behavior is wrong, and for the sake of humanity it *must* stop? Wolves are human too; they are someone's son, brother, or father, perhaps even fiancé or husband.

I go back to Les Halles all the time to see Chex. I hope someday she will find her way off the street. After March, the soup line at Saint-Eustache closed until next winter, and there's a lot less assistance for homeless people over the spring and summer. I tried to persuade Chex to leave, even for one or two nights, and stay at my safe place. But she won't budge from her little patch of sidewalk, like it's her home, even though it has no walls or roof.

Sometimes I go by and see her in the afternoon, and then we walk over to Montesquieu together. People say hi and kiss us on both cheeks. They're glad to see us, and it's always good to see them, but part of me feels guilty because I have a place to stay and Chex and some of the other women don't.

When I see homeless people on the street struggling to survive, I'm overcome with compassion. Sometimes it's as if I can feel their pain, because I have walked in their shoes. I don't have enough to help much, but when I feel their sincerity, I give what I can. *"Outflow determines inflow."* The law that outflow determines inflow is expressed by Jesus: "Give and it will be given to you. Good measure, pressed down, shaken together, running over, will be put into your lap."

My perception of the idea is that the universe will always find a way to balance itself out. For example, if you want to be forgiven, you must forgive; if you want to be loved, you must give love, and so on. What you put out there will find its way back to you.

But be aware this also works on the other end of the scale. If you make your living without regard to the lives you injure, you will be injured; if you act aggressively, you will be treated with aggressiveness, and if you hurt people by starting rumors and gossiping, that will find you as well.

This is why we must always try to consider the consequences of our actions and remember we are only a small piece of a very large puzzle. Believe me, I know, in this day and age, the world is moving so fast around us, it is difficult to always do this, but the more we practice, the easier it becomes.

⚜ ⚜ ⚜

I'd like to start a program asking people to clean out their medicine cabinets every six months and donate medicine they don't need to Agora and places like it. They don't have to be complete boxes, a few pills here and there add up quicker than you might think. Instead of throwing out good medication, it could be put to use by people like Dr. Swartz that really want to help the less fortunate, but don't always have the supplies to do so.

Someday I'd also like to open a shelter with social workers that honestly want to help people get off the streets. I really wish one day the system could be figured out, so the social workers could understand *how* they need to help homeless people, and not just let them dangle from hook to hook, shelter to shelter, and Band-Aid to Band-Aid. Maybe this book could be a start of that.

Perhaps we could start with communication. I was recently told a story about a social worker who spoke many languages, so she was obviously well educated. She really appeared to mean well, and she talked about how she spent all this time doing research on how to help immigrants from a certain country. She got all this information, but failed to pass it on to the other social workers.

They could make a large file, folder, or book and have a different section for each country, with all the detailed information concerning people from that country: what kind of jobs they're allowed to work in France, the special kinds of paperwork they need to file, contact numbers for groups that speak their languages, and non-profit organizations that are set up to help them. Every time someone found a new resource, it could be filed under the appropriate country.

Then when people come in asking for help, they simply pick up the file, folder, or book, find the appropriate information concerning their country, and have a wealth of information at their fingertips. Perhaps they could also have a list of people who are willing to speak their language at Agora and other centers. I would personally be willing to volunteer time at Agora, and other places as well, to help get the ball rolling.

Like I said, I'd never been outside America before I took this trip. Maybe I was a little naive, but I didn't realize how the rest of the world perceives America.

I was told repeatedly by social workers in France: "We don't help Americans, and you're American, so you have to do it on your own." They believed—really believed—America is one of the strongest, wealthiest countries in the world, so if I was born there, I must be strong and wealthy. Sometimes they almost seemed to believe I was superhuman.

Krishnamurti said, "When you call yourself an Indian or a Muslim or a Christian or a European, or anything else, you are being violent. Do you see why it is violent? Because you are separating yourself from the rest of mankind. When you separate yourself by belief, by nationality, by tradition, it breeds violence."

I would walk the streets all night to keep the wolves from attacking me, while women from all these other countries—Russia, Germany, countries in Asia, many African countries, and France—were put up, not just in shelters, but in hostels and hotels by social workers. I would have been happy with a ticket for a shelter.

But they view women who were born in America as different from all of these other women. They honestly expect that you can and will figure it out on your own, and they don't seem to doubt it. They believe America equals money, strength, courage, power, and, apparently easy sex, so if you were born there, you *must* represent all of these. They don't seem to understand that beyond geography, and underneath physical form, we're all the same, regardless of which side of the planet we were born on.

After communication, perhaps we could reeducate people who work with the homeless. No one is superhuman, regardless of where we were born, and women, especially the women, need help finding food and a safe place to stay. We really need social workers as our allies. We need to teach them how to prioritize, that showing up for appointments and getting women off the street is a higher priority than doing research on YouTube and making homeless women sing Christmas songs.

When you walk the street all night to keep the wolves from attacking you, the last thing you want to do is sing. Most of the social workers are very out of touch with the average homeless woman's reality, what she has to do every day and more importantly every night to survive, especially if she doesn't have shelter. Making the social workers live—actually live—in this reality for a brief period of time could be very beneficial and awakening.

Perhaps we could also teach both the social workers and the homeless that they are not their life situation. Most of the social workers I've seen working at Agora confuse the homeless people's life situation with who they are; they judge them and believe that because their life situation is bad, their life is bad. This is unconscious of them; many people have bad life situations, not just homeless people. The social workers should be reinforcing this, but instead they are doing the opposite.

Social workers should be the leaders teaching people in need to separate their life situation from their life, who they are. If they don't, these people will most likely give up, fall into a downward spiral, and possibly become aggressive. I have seen this happen. This is when people appear to start creating their own reality and lose touch with the functioning world.

Eckhart Tolle uses the example of a lake, but after what I have lived through and witnessed other homeless people living through, I believe the example of an ocean is more fitting here.

Imagine the surface of the ocean. There are waves, but these are only on the surface—equivalent to your life situation.

Deep down below on the bottom of the ocean, the water is calm and peaceful. The bottom of the ocean represents your life.

There may be storms on the surface, some worse than others. Perhaps every once in a while there is a tidal wave or the occasional hurricane, and maybe once or twice in your life a tsunami, but they are only your life situation, on the surface. The key is to learn not to confuse the two. You are not your life situation. Your life situation is usually very turbulent, but it is only the surface, it's not your life. Your life is deep within.

Since I started learning about life situations and resisting, it has taken a lot of patience. It doesn't happen overnight. For me it has begun with little glimpses here and there, and they are slowly becoming longer and more frequent. Just because I understand this, it doesn't mean I am able to apply it to all situations every day, but I have the awareness to know I should, and therefore it will come.

⚜ ⚜ ⚜

As for my life situation at this moment, I'm on a very tight budget, but hey, after living on the street, I'm not complaining. I am very happy to have my little safe place, and I have a couple of promising employment possibilities for the future. First of all, a nice English lady I met working at the telemarketing center explained she had a new job; she said she had been TEFL-certified to teach English. The rate of pay is significantly higher and you get to teach people tools they can use to improve their quality of life: communication, job opportunities, and so on. Therefore I'm working on getting TEFL-certified to teach English, but it takes time and, of course, money. And second: well, it involves another passion of mine, writing.

"You don't become good by trying to be good, but by finding the goodness that is already within you, and allowing that goodness to emerge."

I didn't come to Europe to find the love of my life, but Francois is a very close second . . . only to Lester, of course. When you survive on the street with someone, it's like the bond you form surviving a war together. I honestly believe I wouldn't have made it through this without him—his support. Even with everything he was going through for his own survival, he was able to let the goodness inside him flow out. That day he stood up for me at Agora and got me off the street, my heart opened up and let him inside.

"To know another human being in their essence, you don't really need to know anything about them—their past, their history, their story."

One day I woke up with a bad eye infection. I continue to make saline solution when I can't afford the contact lens solution. Francois held warm compresses to my eye while caressing my hair and cheek, singing "Wonderwall," the Oasis song, to me:

> *There are many things that I would like to say to you,*
> *But I don't know how,*
> *Because maybe,*
> *You're gonna be the one that saves me,*
> *I said maybe, you're gonna be the one that saves me,*
> *After all, you're my wonderwall*

Our relationship is evolving, but you must be at a place in your life where you are ready to wake up, for whatever reason you truly want the pain to stop. I believe Francois began the process of waking up before I met him. We continue to help each other grow and evolve—often admitting or pointing out to the other when we are resisting, so we can help each other through it. Francois stays over more and more, and we continue to grow closer and closer.

✤ ✤ ✤

I still don't have a lot of stuff, and when I get something, I know I'll be able to let it go when the time comes. Personal possessions are OK; some things we need for practical purposes. We just need to remember not to identify with them, or with forms.

Paris has some of the most beautiful architectural forms I have ever seen in my life, and they continue to amaze me every day that I discover another layer to this magnificent city, like a rose unfolding as it blooms.

Getting around with the metro is great. There are a lot of stairs and it's hard on my knees, but I can go almost anywhere in the city and suburbs.

It's a challenge to learn French, especially when I don't have a large bank account. It's a very beautiful language, but complex. I recently found a couple of affordable schools, but they only start new classes once a year, so unfortunately I have quite a wait ahead of me, but I continue to study and I am looking for someone to tutor me, or at least do language exchange with.

I love America, but the truth is America is a grand illusion. Everyone believes America is the wealthiest country in the world. Maybe once, long ago, it was, before unconscious politicians had their run. You know the type: They like to start wars and fight for "private greed draped in colors of patriotism." They're more concerned with their personal gain than the welfare of humanity. In reality, the quality of life in France appears to be much higher than in America. I believe France is much wealthier than America, in all the ways that truly matter.

✤ ✤ ✤

Do I regret this experience? No. But would I do it again if I was given a choice? No, even with everything I have learned, at this moment of my life, no. But I am physically still recovering, and mentally attempting to process this new wealth of awareness and evolution I have gained. Perhaps after I physically recover and I'm able to process all of this I will have a different perspective. At this moment, I focus on the positive side.

I have been introduced to many different cultures that I never would have been able to experience in America. I've come to know some incredible people born all over the world, and I've developed a new perspective on life. I have begun to realize that underneath all of the different physical forms, we—all life—really are the same.

My vacation turned out to be a journey, and not just a physical one—a very spiritual one. I believe it has accelerated the awakening process for me. I have gained an astounding amount of awareness, and once I was able to stop resisting, at least part of the time, things just started falling into place. And when I am not able to stop resisting, I have become much more aware of it. Because I'm aware of it, acceptance will eventually come.

Everyone said, "You'll never find work here. So many French people can't find work, and you don't even speak much French." But after two weeks of looking for work, I got my first job interview, and at my first job interview, I was offered work, with a CDD contract.

Then everyone said, "You'll never find an apartment in Paris. There are more people than there are apartments. Why do you think there are so many homeless people here?" Julien even told me that when he worked for a while in England, he kept his apartment in Paris, because he was afraid he wouldn't be able to find another one when he returned. But the first apartment I looked at, I got a lease.

Right here, right now, I believe that France is where I belong. Obviously this is where I am, at this moment in this life, so undoubtedly it is.

"Instead of asking, what do I want from life, a more powerful question is, what does life want from me?"

I found the place where I belong and it's right back here where I started—in France, on this journey labeled life. The difference is: The first time around, France chose me, but the second time around, I chose France, or I accepted the choice life made for me. It was as if

France said, "Oh no, you're not going anywhere, you belong here!" But I was resisting, resisting life. This time around I've realized you don't choose your life, life chooses you.

"Life is the dance and you are the dancer."

The sooner we are able to accept that, the sooner we will be able to start enjoying life. Whenever we are not enjoying life, and we feel pain, we know we are resisting the choice that life has made for us. We must find something to bring us back to the present moment. The more we practice, the easier it becomes to find what works for us. For me, I've learned that sometimes it's as simple as putting one foot in front of the other.

⚜ ⚜ ⚜

I feel the need to leave you with this parable from The Power of Now by Eckhart Tolle. And I sincerely thank everyone in France for welcoming me.

—Ann

"Enlightenment—what is that?"

A beggar had been sitting by the side of the road for over thirty years. One day a stranger walked by. "Spare any change?" mumbled the beggar, mechanically holding out his baseball cap. "I have nothing to give you," said the stranger. Then he asked: "What's that you are sitting on?" "Nothing" replied the beggar. "Just an old box. I have been sitting on it for as long as I can remember." "Ever looked inside?" asked the stranger. "No," said the beggar. "What's the point? There's nothing in there." "Have a look inside," insisted the stranger. The beggar managed to pry open the lid. With astonishment, disbelief, and elation, he saw that the box was filled with gold.

I am the stranger who has nothing to give you and who is telling you to look inside. Not in any box, as in the parable, but somewhere even closer: inside yourself.

—Eckhart Tolle

Special Thanks to

The Webb family; Olivia Gay—without her, you would not be holding this book in your hands; Pascale Kremer for her beautiful writing, editing, and friendship; Reiko, my adopted sister and volunteer social worker; Patrice and Michell Van Eersel; Ruth Marshall for your help writing thirty pages of this book; Gerard; Eckhart Tolle; La Soupe Saint-Eustache and all of the volunteers; Saint-Eustache Church; Albin Michel; Kentucky Scott; Antoine Balas; Louis Lauzin; Saleh; Pierre Abey—founder of Emmaus; Marie and Marc; and Karen Hare.

Thanks to

Marti Gilles, Dr. J. Hamisultane, Paul, Charlene, Caroline H., *Le Monde 2*, M. T. R., Leatitia, L.S., Sarah Edelman, A to S Communication, Oliver, telemarketing company, Chex, Agora, Malmaison, Montesquieu, The women of Montesquieu, Tina, Sara Fults, Father Jonathan, Pierre, Djamila, Alice, Natalie, Pakistan from Malmaison, Gus de Vaumas, Joaquin, Laetitia, Veronique, Isabel, Chloe and Charlette, Jayson and Erin Zilkie, Laurent Madar, La Clairere, and Laurent Codair.